Women's Political Status and Engagement

A Study of Nagaland

Women's Political Status and Engagement

A Study of Nagaland

Moamenla Amer

AKANSHA PUBLISHING HOUSE
NEW DELHI • GUWAHATI • VISAKHAPATNAM

AKANSHA PUBLISHING HOUSE
4649-B/21, Ansari Road
Darya Ganj, New Delhi - 110 002
Ph.: 23263193 / 9811582579 / 09435116718
Fax: 011-23263193
Email: ektabooks@yahoo.com
www.akanshapublishinghouse.com

Women's Political Status and Engagement

First Published 2012

ISBN 978-81-8370-322-2

[The responsibility for the facts stated, conclusions reached etc., is entirely that of the authors. The publisher is not responsible for them, whatsoever.]

PRINTED IN INDIA

Published by Akansha Publishing House, New Delhi and Printed at Harmain Offset, Delhi.

Contents

Acknowledgement

This work would not have been possible without the support and encouragement of many generous people. I am most grateful to all those who went out of their way to provide feedback on initial ideas and commented on certain sections of the work and offered thoughtful comments and suggestions to steer the work in the right direction.

The study also owes a large debt of gratitude to all who helped in conducting the survey for the qualitative portion of this study. I am indebted to the respondents for their participation and willingness to set aside time for this study.

Furthermore, thanks are due to my family members, whose encouragement and support have served as sources of inspiration for this work.

Finally, I owe special thanks to Mrs. T. Atula Ao, my mother, for her loving endurance.

Moamenla Amer

1
Introduction

Historical background of Voting Behaviour Studies

In the late 40's and early 50's, voting behaviour research made a tremendous leap forward with the development of scientific public polls. The first major theory of voting behaviour was advanced by Paul Lazarfeld and his colleagues at Columbia University during the 1940 American Presidential campaign. These studies relied on individual-level measures taken from a random sample of the target population. These studies tended to emphasize the influence of social class on voting. Their model argued that the group and social identifications of individuals were the primary determinants of their voting behaviour. By focusing on the importance of reference group and social networks, the Columbia school introduced an important set of theoretical ideas into the study of voting behaviour (Jeff Manza & Clem Brooks, 1998). This approach, often called the "Columbia" model of voting or the sociological model, maintained that voting decisions are based on social group identity (based on characteristics such as class, race and religion), education and occupational status (Chris Lawrence, 2001).

The study of voting behaviour made a major scientific advancement with the publication by Angus Campbell, *et al.*

of "*The American Voter*" in 1960. They built on the work of Berelson, et al, and advanced a model of vote choice called the 'Michigan or socio-psychological' model. According to Campbell, *et al.* (1960), individual voting choice is determined by his or her party identification. In their words, the authors describe party identification as a 'firm but not immovable attachment'.

Donald P Green, *et al.* (2000) see party identification as a kind of social group identification. Partisans identify with the type of people popularly associated with one party or another. This provides a more substantive definition of party identification, without contesting the basic empirical findings that it is strongly influential, stable, but can be temporarily overcome by short- term considerations Party identification were supposedly formed early in life, often inherited from ones parents and then generally reinforced by habitual support for ones preferred party. These party identifications filters individual's views of the political world, providing them with a means not only for making voting decisions but also for interpreting and evaluating political phenomena (Richard Rose, 2000).

Over time, subsequent scholars have depicted various aspects of *The American Voter's* depiction of voter's psychology. Of particular relevance, their depiction of party identification has been disputed in several ways. Some scholars argue that voters are not the habitual partisan voters implied in the psychological model. Heinz Eulau, *et al.* (2004) argues that voters are to a greater or lesser extent susceptible to the influence of more short term and contingent factors such as campaign events, issues, and candidate appeals. In particular, the perceived governing competence of candidates and political parties often weighs heavily on voters choice. This shift from long term predisposition to short term evaluation, according to the authors, has been facilitated in part by the phenomenon of "cognitive mobilization", a supposed enhancement of the political independence and intelligence of voters who are both better educated and better informed than earlier generation.

While information might be subject to some 'partisan bias', variations in national conditions and personal well-being modify voters' self-identities (Achen, C.H, 1992). Few voters approach the election with such sociological or psychological predispositions. Many individuals base their decisions on the issue and candidates of the campaign and the influence of friends, colleagues, and other political cue-givers, which produces an individualization of voting choice. This shift in the source of voting cues leads to an eclectic and egocentric pattern of political decision making, as voters base their electoral decisions on policy preference, performance judgments or candidates images (Richard Rose, 2000).

In Europe the introduction of the concept of party identification has proved rather problematic. This is mainly due to the development of the multi-party format of European politics and the presence of mass cleavage-parties. Such a development appeared formidable barriers to conceiving party identification as an individual attitude (John Bartle and Paolo Bellucci, 2006).

However, in essence, these studies still provide the core of the concepts and models used in contemporary voting research. Most empirical work since the publication of *The American Voter* has at least implicitly incorporated their model. The psychological approach of the *American Voter* was exported to other democracies through a series of collaborative cross-national research projects. Although these studies often illustrated the peculiarities of American electoral politics and thus the diffulty of exporting American concepts, researchers often observed a functional equivalence between Europe and America in the central elements of the psychological model.

The influence of this approach was so pervasive that party identification- and the model it represents- became the central theoretical concept in electoral research (Richard Rose, 2002).

Theoretical development of election studies in developed countries, especially the United States, has inspired an upward trend in election studies in India. Studies on voting behaviour, notably the Columbia and Michigan studies, have had an impact on studies in India relative to determining what the important research questions are. Party identification, issues, candidates, campaigns, socio-economic status of voters, and other areas have been recognized as important realms for studies in voting behaviour. But because of the peculiar elements that are characteristic of Indian society, such as caste, electoral studies in India have unique features (Norio Kondo, 2007).

Concept of Voting Behaviour

The traditional approach of studying politics underwent change owing to the behavioural movement. Instead of studying state and other political institutions, behaviouralists emphasized upon the efficacy and relevance of studying observed political behavior underlying particular institutional and legal arrangements.[1]

Today the term voting behaviour connotes more than the examination of voting records, compilation of voting statistics and computation of electoral shifts. The concept has acquired a new dimension with a broader meaning. Now it is treated as a sub-field or considered a sub-area of political behaviour.[2]

Voting behaviour is concerned with finding out series of psychological, cultural, social and economic considerations that go into individual's act of voting. Such a study offers an opportunity to gain insights into the mental process of the citizens and the human dimensions of a political system.[3] It is one such study that tries to explain the determinants and consequences of citizen's participation in democracy. It seeks to explain why people choose to support a particular party or candidate when voting at elections and more importantly, what demographic and socioeconomic factors can explain what motivates or activate citizens to vote.

Over the years, the study of voting behaviour has come to command an important position in political analysis. This is because voting provides one of the richest sources of information about the interaction between individuals, society and politics. Through such a study one can learn important lessons about the nature of the political system and gain insight into the process of social and political change.[4]

Voting behaviour of the individuals, which reflects their political behaviour, can be studied, explained and observed at the time of elections when they cast their votes to choose their representatives who govern the country on their behalf.[5] Such a study helps in investigating the nature and extent of participation of people in politics. It also throws ample light on the multidimensional facets of citizen's participation in the political process.

Voter's level of participation in the political process is influenced by many factors. One of the most common generalizations regarding participation in politics is that levels of socio-economic status affect citizen's involvement in politics. This has been confirmed by a number of studies where participation, voting and socioeconomic status have been shown to be strongly correlated. It has been found that men vote more than women, the better educated more than the less educated, urban residents more than rural, the middle aged more than the young and old.[6]

According Verba & Nie (1972), socio-economic status of the voters is the most important key to understanding politics in a democratic state. The common explanation of this tendency is that political participation generally requires political resources and that those with higher socio-economic status can more readily afford such investment. Zipp, *et al.* (1982) state that, "Due to less education, more restricted occupation-related learning experience, greater social isolation, lower status persons, compared with higher status persons are less interested in politics, are less aware of the need for or possible benefits of participation, feel less politically efficacious, less often possess those social and political skills and have less time, money and energy to expend in political participation".

On a similar line, M.Ramchander & K.Lakshmi (1993) in *Women and Politics: A Study in Political Participation,* states that people with urban orientations, high social status, high income earnings, high occupational status, and having greater exposure to mass media and with high degree of political interest and information are likely to be more participative than those who have less of the above. Voting behaviour is also determined by the political attitudes, assumptions, policy preference and partisan loyalties of individuals and the political and institutional context within which they cast their votes in an election.[7]

In politically advanced country, the voting choice is preferred mainly in terms of the ideological programme and politics of the rival parties and candidates, while on the other hand, in a politically under-developed country, even basic issues are decided in terms of traditional criterion of the states and power influence of the rivals in the field.[8] Although socio-economic and the demographic factors are considered by most scholars to be the strongest predictors of voting behaviour, other considerations also play a part in determining who is likely to participate or abstain. Numerous studies have shown that voting behaviour depends not only on the personal attributes of electors themselves, but also on the social environment in which the voter is embedded. In other words, voting is not only a function of citizen's personal attributes, but also of attributes of their social contexts.

Against this background, the present study will examine the different dimensions of women's voting behaviour in Nagaland. Citizen's participation through voting is still the heart of democratic process, yet, participation is not a single, undifferentiated entity.[9] Restated, to gauge level of citizen's participation based solely on voting ignores the influence of other modes of political behaviour. Therefore, going beyond the act of voting, the study examines women's participation in other modes of electoral activities as well.

Need of the Study

There can be no better justification for undertaking a work of this kind, in a state where half of the population of the state is still left on the periphery of the political process. This work explores largely uncharted terrain with regard to voting behaviour of women voters in Nagaland, an area that has not gained much attention. Keeping in mind the low political profile of Naga women, it is pertinent to understand the different aspects of their voting behaviour, so that the right policies and strategies can be framed. A study of this kind may also help to understand and identify the factors hindering women's breakthrough in politics and draw data on the level of women's political mobility, their level of political awareness and the extent of women voters influence on the outcome of elections in Nagaland.

Data and method

The present work was undertaken to address the different aspects of voting behaviour of women voters in Nagaland. Since no evaluative research has been done till date on the subject under study, the work depends entirely on analysis of data from the field and Government election records.

The data used for the analysis is based on a representative sample of women voters in 2008-2009, just after the 2008 Assembly Election. It is usual in voting behaviour studies in India to take up for study, the voting behavior of one rural and one urban unit for the purpose of comparison. Accordingly, four towns were selected to represent the urban area. They are, Kohima, Dimapur, Mokokchung and Tuensang. To represent the rural area, four villages were selected. They are Thezima (Kohima district), Chare (Tuensang district), Ungma (Mokchung district) and Ghaspani (Dimapur district).

The target sample is drawn from the above four towns and four villages. As it is practically not possible to make direct observation of every individual in the population, a representative sample was selected to make inferences for the entire women population. The selection of the sample was made on the basis of random sampling. Accordingly, women who are eligible to vote, 18 years and above were selected for the study sample. In the selection of the sample, the following factors were considered:

- A representative sample of eligible women voters residing in the urban areas and rural areas were represented in the sample.
- All levels of socio-economic backgrounds were represented in the sample.

Individuals in the sample list were classified according to their age, educational qualifications, marital status, occupational status, and place of residence, i.e., (urban-rural). Income variable was not included because the responses were too insignificant to allow firm conclusions to be drawn. The respondents were divided into four age groups of 18-29, 30-44, 45-59 and 60 and above years. After measuring their respective levels of education, the respondents were divided into - illiterate, non-matric, under-graduate, and graduate and above categories. The respondents were classified as either married or unmarried. Occupational status was similarly reported as a categorical variable, there being four groups-service, professionals, cultivators, and non-earners. To maintain a comparative perspective, data concerning the geographical distribution of the respondents was classified according to the type of settlement they live in, i.e., their place of residence was coded as either urban or rural. For the present analysis, electoral activities are indicated by five activities - voting, campaigning for a candidate, attending election meetings, party membership and political discussions.

Field work was mainly carried out through face-to-face interviews. The response rate of the survey, calculated as the number of completed interviews is 85.39 per cent, resulting in a sample survey of 304 respondents. The precise level of representivity of this sample for the entire women population of Nagaland cannot be estimated. However, the accuracy and consistency is ensured by the relatively large size of the sample.

Primary data was collected through questionnaire schedule, personal interview and participant observation. The questionnaire was developed after an extensive collection and review of both primary and secondary literature. The questions for the questionnaire have been framed empirically, with both open and closed format questions. To aid in the interpretation of results, the questionnaire contained a diverse range of topics. It elicited detailed information from the respondents relating to their socio-economic background, their participation in voting and other indices of electoral activities and information relating to the respondents knowledge about politics.

Apart from the respondents to whom questionnaire was addressed, women from various walks of life were interviewed to supplement and enrich the interpretation of results obtained from the questionnaire. Observation was another primary tool used to confirm information obtained through questionnaire schedule, personal interviews and secondary data sources.

The secondary data sources included relevant published and unpublished books, reports, articles, official records, such as, Statistical Handbooks, census data from the Directorate of Census, relevant Government publications from the Directorate of Economics and Statistics, State Election Commission Report, State Assembly Secretariat, various reports, journal article's, academic conference papers, journalistic outputs, etc. These sources supplemented information obtained through primary data. All sources are listed in the bibliography.

In most of the cases, percentages were calculated in interpreting the findings and presented in the form of tables, figures, and charts, representing various aspects of the study. In order to avoid subjective judgments, effort has been made to make the analysis as factual, empirical and impartial as possible.

Overview of the Chapters

The book is organized into six chapters that coincide with the structure of the study.

Chapter one details the historical background of voting behaviour studies. This is followed by a discussion on the concept of voting behaviour. Thereafter the need of the study is specified. The chapter also details the methodology applied to collect and analyze data, which was best suited to respond to the present work.

Chapter two aims to contextualize debates over the political status of women within the complex political and cultural space in Nagaland. The structural, institutional and situational factors in the context of women's political status are discussed. As participation in social organization is considered a major antecedent of electoral participation, women's involvement in social organization is also examined.

Chapter three highlights the socio-economic profile of the women electorate. It also includes an examination of the association between the various socio-economic factors and women's participation in voting and the reasons for voting and non-voting.

Chapter four deals with women's participation in different dimensions of electoral activities beyond voting. This is followed by a discussion on the factors that influence their extent of electoral participation. Finally, the chapter reflects upon the barriers to women's participation in the electoral process.

Chapter five deals with the knowledge dimension of women voters. The chapter examines how well informed the women voters are about politics, what factors influence their level of awareness about politics and whether their level of political awareness influences their participation in electoral activities.

Chapter six draws findings and conclusion from the previous analysis. The conclusion addresses how these findings can be used in efforts to engage women in the political process.

NOTES

1. Sushila, P. (1994) *Women Political Elite: Search for Identity*. Printwell, Jaipur, p.2.
2. *Ibid,* p.1.
3. Z.M. Quaraishi (1979) *Elections and State Politics in India: A Case Study of Kashmir*, Sundeep Prakashan, Delhi, p.236. Trust Publications, May 12-18, Vol.XXXVI, NO.19.
4. S.Goswami (2001) "Changing Electoral Trends." *Economic and Political Weekly*, A Sameeksha Trust Publications, May 12-18, Vol.XXXVI, N0.19.

5. S.C.Kashyup. (ed) (1971) *Elections and Electoral Reforms in India,* New Delhi, p.23.

6. S.M.Lipset. (1960) *Political Man: The Social Bases of Politics.* Johns Hopkins University Press, Maryland.

7. Seymour Martin Lipset. (ed) (1995) *Encyclopedia of Democracy,* Vol. IV, p.1346. Routledge, London.

8. S.P.Verma & C.P.Bhambri (eds) (1967) *Elections and Political Consciousness in India.* Meenakshi, Meerut, p.20.

9. Sidney Verba, Ahmed, B., & X.Bhatt.,A. (1971) *Caste, Race and Politics.* Beverly Hills, Sage, p.29.

2

Political Status of Women in Nagaland

Introduction

One of the most trying issues in electoral studies is the discourse of women's exclusion in the electoral process. This chapter aims to contextualize debates over the political status of women within the complex political and cultural space in Nagaland. The structural, institutional and situational factors in the context of women's political status are discussed. The chapter concludes by a discussion on women's participation in social organizations and whether such organizations present opportunities for women to mobilize for greater political voice and provide political platforms to engage in gender inclusive politics.

Political Status of Women

Political status can be defined as the degree of equality and freedom enjoyed by women in shaping and sharing of power and in the value given by society to this role of women.

Indian constitution grants women full political rights, equal to those of men. Women can vote, run for office and hold ministerial and higher positions. According to the Reports of the Committee on Status of Women, three main indicators can be used to assess political status of women [2], viz., (i) participation in the political process as voters and candidates in elections; (ii) political attitudes such as awareness, commitment and involvement in politics and autonomy in political action and behaviour; and (iii) their impact on the political process.

The Naga women in the recent decades have successfully pushed for increased participation in many fields of activities. However, one area where Naga women's participation is conspicuously missing is in the political arena. The context of the political status and role of the Naga women continues to be an open question. Relative to their share in the population, they remain outsiders in politics. Even after more than four decades of statehood, there has been no woman member in the State Legislative Assembly. This reinforces the perception that electoral politics in Nagaland continue to be dominated by men. A domination that should not really be, because of the almost equal proportion of the two genders in the population. If half of the states enfranchised population is kept out of the political structures of the state, one cannot talk of democracy. The Naga women's ongoing demand to participate equally in decision-making is based on the ground that representative democracy means equal opportunities for participation in politics of all citizens regardless of their sex. The parity representation of women is also indicative of justice and equality of the society.

In the North East, one finds two simultaneous democratic institutions at work, a modern democratic system vis-à-vis a traditional system among the hill tribes.[3] Despite the fact that modern system of governance has been ushered in since Nagaland got Statehood on 1st December, 1963, yet age old traditional practices and values prevails. In Nagaland, patriarchy appears to control all institutions of the society, be it the modern or the traditional institutions. The reason why there are no women in the State Legislature till date is not that women lose the election, but only few women decide to run for elections. For women to be elected to the state legislature, they have to go through many barriers. First of all they have to decide to run for elective office. This itself will be a difficult decision for many women, conditioned by years of patriarchy. The decision to contest in election will be influenced by many factors like personal ambition, availability of resources, prevailing societal attitude, and the political environment. Secondly, they have to be nominated by a political party as a candidate to run for political office. Generally nomination is determined by the party leaders who are usually male. Even if women are selected by the party, their chance of getting nominated in winning constituencies is difficult. This could be the biggest hurdle for women getting entry to the legislature. And lastly they have to be selected by the voters to become legislators.

Traditionally, political parties are considered be the most important formal political structures that determine the level of women's participation and representation in politics. This is mainly because they remain the gatekeepers to elective office. Yet, political parties in Nagaland appear to be male dominated. They have not genuinely taken up the issue of political participation by women, either inside the party through leadership posts or outside the party through candidacy on electoral lists. This is reflected by the near total absence of women in party leadership and thereby influence over party decision. The few women members are largely auxiliaries and supporters of male leadership.

Some of the women party activists expressed dissatisfaction with the gendered division of labour within the party structure. The activities of women in party organization, they opine, are more or less restricted to auxiliary and support roles. Political parties frequently mobilize them to support the party men. Besides casting their votes, their electoral activities is just confined to preparing meals for party events or home visitation, which in many cases, are to distribute material goods to the prospective voters. Women committees exist just for the purported purpose of activating female voters. It does not develop women political cadres. Some have even questioned the internal democracy of the party. These narratives reveal that the general commitment of the political parties in Nagaland to the advancement of women is very much of a token nature.

The number of women candidates sponsored by political parties is also low. Therefore, women resort to contesting election as Independent candidate. The reluctance of political parties to nominate women is probably the single biggest barrier to women being elected, because without nomination they do not have the party machinery behind them. So long as the political parties refrain from supporting and promoting women's candidacies, the representation of women will continue to lag behind men. Therefore it is important to examine who actually controls the nomination process. One of the reasons for the historically high women's representation in the Scandinavian countries is that women's organizations have consistently asked the question: who controls the nomination process? Subsequently they have demanded 50 per cent women on the nomination committees 5.

On the other hand, the traditional institutions around which the Naga social and political life revolves have never recognized the rights of women as primary decision makers. A case in point is the Naga Hoho, considered as the apex decision-making body of the Naga people and is represented by different Naga tribes. Till date it has no woman representative. At the grassroots level, the Village Council is the highest decision-making body. It is represented by all the clans in the village. However, traditionally women are still not allowed to take part in the decision-making of the Village Council. These institutions, modern as well as traditional, are considered to be democratic bodies, which are supposed to be a means for all citizens to be equally represented or involved.

Unlike their male counterparts, women do not receive positive reinforcement from the society at large for participation in politics. Naga women live with an identity of being marginal especially in politics. Men dictate if not control the public spaces for women and this becomes quiet prominent when the subject is politics. The dominance of power in dictating who participates in politics is clearly evident by the opposition to the 33 per cent reservation of seats for women in local bodies – Municipal and Town Councils- on grounds of cultural rationales and unexamined assumptions. The ongoing opposition to the bill is only one example to illustrate the extent to which women's right to participate in politics is often abused if not sterilized by the so called 'cultural guards' of our society. This indicates the existence of biases against women taking part in electoral activities.

The following are some of the responses given on the political status of Naga women by the women respondents:

> *"The political status of women in Nagaland in terms of equality and opportunities has not changed much".*
>
> *"Even though we talk about equality given to both men and women, our society is still headed by men in all areas".*

These are just two examples of narratives given by the women respondents, which illustrate the low political status of women in Nagaland. The literature on democracy takes as its starting point the notion that political equality involves some degree of equality in participation, and it treats the systematic absence of particular social groups as a self evident failing of democracy. The link between women's representation and democracy should be self evident.[4]

If the definition of democracy allows for participation of different groups in the society, then it cannot thrive by excluding women both in the context of participation as well as representation. In the context of Nagaland, what seems debatable is whether democratic process can flourish in the current dispensation, where politics is characterized as male, excluding women. Though women in Nagaland are seen as equal members of the community, they are not held equal as political subjects. Equality is hardly achieved when some groups have so much leverage than others.[5] Since women in Nagaland represent almost half of the population of the state, if they do not enjoy an equal political status with men, both as participants as well as representatives, the society can hardly be called democratic.

Thus, it appears that despite the introduction of modern democratic systems for more than four decades and notwithstanding the legal provisions of equality enshrined in the Indian constitution, political status of Naga women has not improved. The political status of Naga women remains by and large low-profiled and unrecognized. They enjoy the right to vote and to be elected to decision- making positions, but these legal provisions have meant little by way of enhancing their political status. Without a meaningful participation and representation of women in politics, built on the principles of parity, it will be impossible to build a democratic civil society.

Women Voters and the Women Candidates

Though elections in Nagaland have at times been held with evidence of wide spread electoral corruption, such as vote buying, vote rigging, voter intimidation and out breaks of violence in polling places, official statistics indicate a general increase in the turnout of women voters. This shows that the women voters participate equally at the ballot box with men. This scenario positively encourages one to think that women in Nagaland are moving ahead in terms of participation in electoral process. However, their high participation in voting has not been accompanied by a corresponding rise in number of women as contestants, elected representatives and members of government.

This trend of high turnout by women voters leads to an important theoretical question, i.e., whether women voters are exercising their basic political right of voting independently. It is pertinent to mention here that the principle of one individual one vote is a political right given to all citizens in a democracy. The exercise of this right by individual citizens is an important indicator of their response to the political rights conferred on them by the constitution and it also constitute an indicator of citizen's political awareness. This question remains to be probed further in the consequent chapters.

Table 2.1 shows the percentage of men and women who voted at each of the Assembly Election that took place in a period of approximately four decades (1964-2008). The first and the ninth Assembly Election has been left out of the table due to non-availability of data by gender.

A number of general inferences can be made from table 2.1 regarding the voting behavior of the women voters. The data reflects a marked fluctuation in the number of women voters registered as voters, between high and low, in each successive Assembly Elections in Nagaland. From 46.97 per cent in 1969, the number of women voters has increased to 48.83 per cent in 2008. There has been an increase of women voters by 1.85 per cent in a period of more than four decades.

The data also shows that the women voters tend to vote more than the male voters. This shows that the male politicians are voted to power on the women vote. This fact also leads one to assume that, if female voters vote for female candidates, they can be voted to political office. The reason

Table 2.1
Gender Difference in Voting (in percentage) in Nagaland, 1969-2008

Year	*Voters*			*Voters who voted*			*% of votes*		*Difference in votes polled by male and female*
	M	*F*	*T*	*M*	*F*	*T*	*M*	*F*	
1969	93829	83102	176931	72196	67132	139328	76.94	80.78	3.84
1974	221223	173847	395070	161164	136484	297648	72.85	78.50	5.65
1977	214812	183223	398035	176666	154795	331461	82.24	84.48	2.24
1982	330290	266163	596453	240422	203500	443922	72.79	76.45	3.66
1987	319529	262772	582301	266033	225891	491924	83.25	85.96	2.71
1988-89	320611	261805	582416	273574	225248	498822	85.32	86.03	0.71
1993	427450	387355	814805	387448	347494	734942	90.64	89.70	0.94
2003	529517	485363	1014880	474181	417316	891497	89.54	85.98	3.56
2008	666391	635875	1302266	573021	549362	1122383	85.98	86.39	0.41

Source: Report on the General Elections to Nagaland Legislative Assembly.

why it is important for women to be elected to political office is not only for reason of parity. Women elected to political office can generate interest in politics among women. This is substantiated by a number of research findings which report that visible female candidates can trigger political interest on a wide range of political activities among women.[6]

Where there are more female politicians in office, women are more likely to discuss and participate in politics as they become more inspired by the activities of visible role models.[7] An emulative mechanism might exert some positive effects. As Burns et al. argued, 'visible women in politics might function as role models and carry a kind of symbolic significance-sending the message to women citizens that politics is an inclusive domain, open to them'. [8]

However, electoral success continues to elude women. While improvements in women's educational and professional status may be a stimulus for women's empowerment, this is clearly not sufficient to win elected office. In the electoral history of Nagaland, spanning a period of more than four decades, thirteen women candidates have contested, but all were repeatedly defeated. The number of women candidates contesting for the State Legislature has been extremely discouraging. It has just been 0.73 per cent of the total number of male candidates. A better comparative assessment can be had by looking at Table 2.2, which highlights the number of male and female candidates contesting in the Assembly Election from 1969-2008.

In order to examine whether women voters vote for women candidates, the survey respondents were asked an open-ended question, as to why they had voted/not voted for the female candidate in the Assembly Election of 2008. An overwhelming number of the women respondents (65 %) did not vote for the women candidates. This reflects the fact that women candidates in Nagaland are yet to win the approval of not just the electorate as a whole, but also from the women voters as well. Just 35 per cent of the respondents voted for the women candidates. This may imply the possibility that the women voter's exhibits prejudice against women candidates.

Table 2.2
Male/Female Contestants in State Assembly Elections, 1969-2008

Year of Election	*Total No of seats*	*Total No. of contestants who contested election*			*Difference of % Male/Female*
		Male	*Female*	*No of women elected*	
1969	40	142	2	Nil	1.40
1974	60	219	-	-	-
1977	60	201	-	-	-
1982	60	245	-	-	-
1987	60	214	3	Nil	1.40
1988-89	60	140	-	-	-
1993	60	177	1	Nil	0.56
2003	60	222	3	Nil	1.35
2008	60	214	4	Nil	1.87
Total	60	1774	13	Nil	0.73

Source: Report on the General Elections to Nagaland Legislative Assembly

The open-ended response was difficult to classify into neat categories because the answers covered a wide and varied spectrum. However some of the respondents expressed something that could be directly classified as having to do with their preconceived notions of gender role stereotypes. Some responses related to the respondent's assessment of the performance and capability of the women candidates.

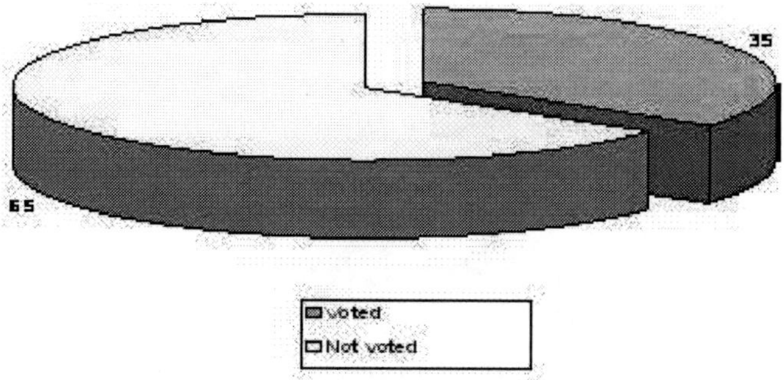

Fig 2.1 Women who Voted/Not Voted for Woman Candidate in Assembly Election, 2003

According to the respondents who did not vote for women candidates, some said that the "male candidates were better than the female candidates". This view can partly be explained by the fact that, voters in patriarchal societies are more likely to perceive women as less qualified than men to run for public office. Since the 1960s many scholars have advanced the view that women are influenced by the stereotypical notion that 'politics is a man's world' [9] and more recent studies have also confirmed the view that women still suffer from a self-perception of being unsuitable to compete in the political environment.[10] (Fox and Lawless, 2004)

The effect of a gendered socialization should not be underestimated. Generally, gender-role stereotyping is still prevalent and accepted in our society. Women and men are conditioned by society to play different roles. Women's main role is largely deemed to be in the household. Leadership role is still conceptualized as a preserve of men in our society. They are projected as leaders and women the followers both in the domestic and public life. In fact politics and women are seen as each other's anti thesis. Therefore, the electorate as a whole may perceive women as less qualified and less suited for politics than men. Such perspective is echoed in the following statements:

> *"The idea that males are superior to females is deeply embedded in the mind of the voters. They fail to consider the qualities of female candidates and vote for male candidates irrespective of whether he would make a good leader or not".*

> *"When it comes to election, leave alone men, women also do not have trust in women candidates".*

Such prevailing attitude towards women contributes to the lack of confidence that many voters have in women candidates. Such perceptions towards women as political leaders become a major barrier to the election of women to elective office. According to another woman respondent:

> *"I did not vote for the woman candidate because I feel that the women's place is in the home bringing up the children".*

This response can similarly be taken as the respondent's explicit reference to the traditional conception of gender roles to explain why women do not vote for women candidates. Such responses highlight the fact that perhaps due to their cultural learning, which teaches that men are the leaders, women almost invariably vote for the male candidates. Such lack of support for women candidates by the respondents may also be a reflection of the predominant perception of women's role in Naga society. Therefore, those few women who may have an interest to contest may be reluctant to do so and if they do contest, they may fail to attract sufficient support to win.

Some of the women said that they were not sure about the candidate's ability. Others felt that the women candidates were not well known. This could mean that involvement in community, public affairs, becomes an important criterion for a candidate's selection by the voters.

Some of the women interviewed expressed the opinion that political parties in Nagaland accord low priority to women's candidature. Women often find their efforts to break into politics marginalized by the failure of the parties to support their viability as candidates. Though political parties have women wings, women are often not recruited to run for elective office. For instance, in the Assembly Election of 2003, out of the three women candidates just one of them managed to contest on a party platform.

Another practice of the political party which marginalizes women from politics is that, those few women aspirants they nominate are given ticket in constituencies where the party has less chance of winning. The NPF party in the Assembly Election of 2003 has nominated its lone women candidate to contest against a seasoned politician like S.C. Jamir.

Despite their low political profile women have expressed a desire to be part of the decision-making process and to be visible in public life, breaking the stereotypes that politics in Nagaland is for men only. This is substantiated by the optimistic views given by the respondents about women's role in the political arena and women's future political prospects.

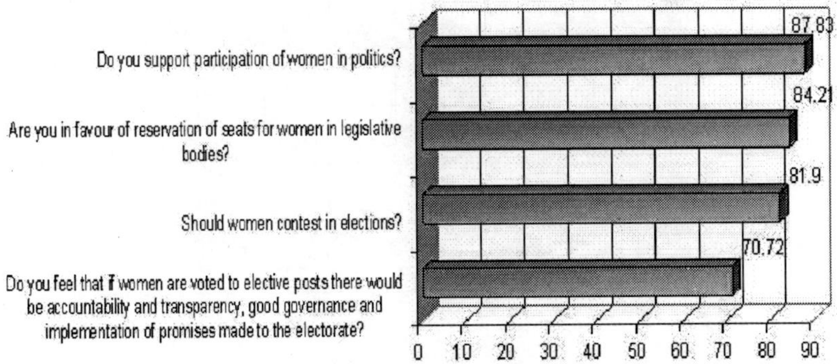

Fig 2.2. Women's Perception of their Political Role

As summarized in Fig 2.2, about 81.9 per cent of them said that women should contest in elections. Around 84.21 per cent of them are in favour of reservation of seats for women in legislative bodies. Some (70.72 %) feel that if women are voted into elective posts there would be accountability and transparency, good governance and implementation of promises made to the electorate. Around 87.83 per cent of them support participation of women in politics. It is clear that women respondents recognize that women have an important contribution to make to political life of the state.

The respondents also identified a range of structural and attitudinal measures in order to enhance the number of women in politics. As reflected in Fig 2.3, the respondents identifies the society (91.78 %), political parties (87.52 %), Government (77.3 %), political interest (74.34 %) and women themselves (72.04 %), as measures to enhance women's visibility in politics in the state.

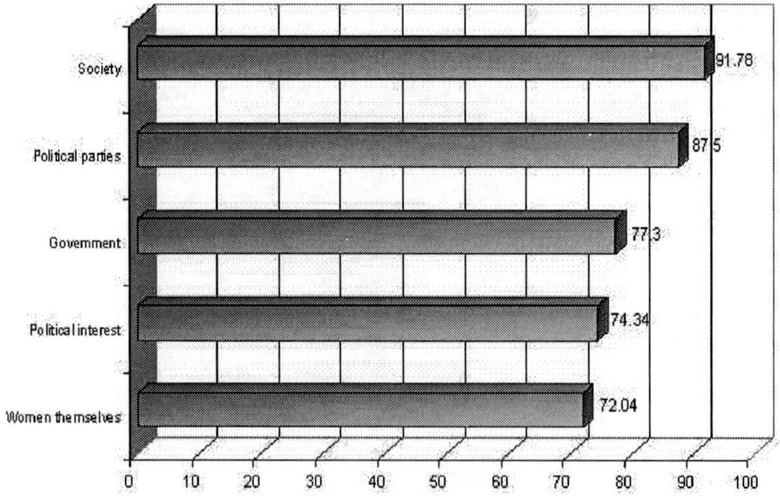

Fig 2.3. Measures to Enhance Women's Presence in Politics

For those voters who voted for women candidates, majority of them expressed that women candidates can represent them and the women issues. The presence of women in elective office could increase respect for women especially in politics and it may also be a form of recognition of the equal status of women in the society. More importantly, the presence of women in elective office could serve to raise the aspirations of other women.

Basing on the responses given by the women respondents, it can be interpreted to mean that the barriers to women gaining entry into elective office lie not so much with the electorate, but on how society as a whole perceive women in public role. In fact, systematic cross national evidence has shown that egalitarian attitudes towards women as political leaders are strongly related to the proportion of women elected to public office.[11] Women are more likely to emerge as candidates in states that established an early pattern of electing women to the state legislature, support women's participation in public affairs, and do not have a tradition of sex-discrimination in income, or gender disparities in educational achievement.[12] Therefore, a more egalitarian public portrayal relating to women's political participation may plausibly influence both whether women in Nagaland are willing to come forward as candidates for elective office and whether they can win.

The political parties too have an important role to play in bringing about a change in the political status of women. The first responsibility of political parties is to accept and than support the idea that women have a significant role to play in the party as leaders, candidates and ultimately, as elected representatives.

Participation in Social Organizations

Individual's participation in electoral activities cannot be isolated from participation in social organization. This requires us to examine and understand the social dimension of voting behaviour. For many women participation in social organizations may be the only means of public participation. In other words, participation in social organization could possibly create alternative public spaces for women outside the party and other formal political structures, which are all male dominated.

Studies in political science have shown that participation in social organization might expose members to politics. One reason why organizational membership might be expected to affect political competence and activity is that the members of such organizations receive training for participation within the organization. [13] Being a member of social organization makes many demands in terms of the ability to communicate and to organize events and meetings. It may, by that token, mean acquiring decision-making skills and participation skills. The various social organizations, not only aim to achieve certain goals, but in the process of doing so, may also help draw women into the political life, encourage the members to become more active in the political process. By being members of social organization, women may enhance their social status and recognition.

Though women in Nagaland are almost invisible in the political arena, they play a central role in the often unrecorded politics that usually takes place at the juncture between larger institutional politics and women's daily experiences. In Nagaland there are a number of voluntary organizations where women's participation is quiet visible, like the NMA (Naga Mothers Association), the Watsu Mungdang, and the Naga Women HoHo, to mention a few. Some of these women's organizations have been able to publicly broach different issues, ranging from women's representation in public office to issue of corruption. They are also credited with keeping up the pressure on the State Government for setting up the State Women's Commission, which was set up in 2006.

One of the most high profile initiatives in the peace negotiation was undertaken by a women's association, the NMA. They played a major role in the signing of the Cease-Fire Agreement between the Government of India and the

Nationalist Socialist Council of Nagaland (NSCN) on 25th July 1997. Their initiative demonstrated the level of concern about the social and political crisis confronting the state at that time and an eagerness to participate equally with their male counterpart in public life.

Taking into consideration the issue discussed above, the role of women NGO's in motivating women to participate in politics becomes critical. Indeed feminists analyses of democratization document that women active in NGO's have taken the advantage of the political openings to mobilize, to insist on their inclusion in the democratization process, to demand that women's issues be added by the political system and to shape public discourse .[12] They can mobilize for greater political voice and provide a platform for women to demand for gender-inclusive politics.

Conclusion

The present chapter has presented an overview of the political status of women within the complex political and cultural terrains of the state. It has touched on a number of structural, institutional and situational factors that contribute to the low political status of women. Although the aforementioned factors certainly play a major role, the persisting impact of the culture of the society on women's participatory behavior should not be underestimated. As participation in social organization is considered a major antecedent of electoral participation women's involvement in social organizations have been examined.

NOTES

1. ICSSR, Report of 1975, *Towards Equality*, National Committee on Status of Women, Allied Publishers, New Delhi, p.103.
2. *Ibid,* p.104.
3. S.D.Hazarika. "Political Participation of Women and the Dilectics of 73rd Amendment." *The Indian Journal of Political Science,* Vol.LXVII, No 2, April-June, 2006.

4. Robert Inglehart., et al. (2001) "Gender Equality and Democracy." *Teaching and Research Review*, Issue 5, winter, 2005.

5. Anne Phillips. (1995) *The Politics of Presence.* Claredon Press Oxford.

6. David.E.Campbell., and Christina Wolbrecht, "See Jane Run:Women politicians as Role Models for Adolescents," *The Journal of Politics*, Vol, N.2, May 2006, pp, 233-247.

7. Wolbrecht,C., and David Campbell. (2007) "Leading by Example:Female Members of Parliament as Political Role Models" *American Journal of Political Science*, 51(4):921-39

8. Burns. *et al.* (2001) *The Private Roots of Public Action*, Cambridge, MA: Harvard University Press.

9. Rapoport, Ronald (1981) 'The Sex in Political Persuading: Where the Structuring Principle Works', *American Journal of Political Science* 25, February: 32–48.

10. Fox, Richard and Jennifer Lawless (2004) 'Entering the Arena? Gender and the Decision to Run for Office', *American Journal of Political Science* 48(2): 264–80.

11. Pippa Norris & R.Inglehart (2001) "Cultural Obstacles to Equal Representation," *Journal of Democracy* 12(3):127-140.

12. David Hill. (1981) "Political Culture on Female Political Representation." *Journal of Politics* 43 (1): 159-65.

13. Almond, G., and S.Verba. (1963) *The Civic Culture: Political Attitudes and Democracy in Five Nations.* Princeton University Press, New Jersey.

14. Linda Racioppi and Katherine O'Sullivan See, Engendering Democratic Transition from Conflict: Women's Inclusion in Northern Irelands Peace Process, *Comparative Politics*,Vol 38 Number 2, January 2006,189-208.

3

Socio-economic Variables and Voting Participation

Introduction

This chapter highlights the socioeconomic profile of the women respondents interviewed during the fieldwork. Thereafter, an analysis is made to find out the association, if any, between the socioeconomic variables and the voting participation of the women voters.

The study of Voting Behaviour is mainly based upon finding the important factors that motivate people to vote one way or another. It is apparent that voter's decision to turnout or to abstain is potentially subject to a number of particular influences. According to the literature on turnout, electoral participation and abstention varies across socio-demographic groups. Factors like age, marital status, education, occupation, income and place of residence play an important role in explaining the nature and extent of individual's engagement in electoral politics. They are believed to have a direct effect on the vote and can indirectly affect different aspects of voting behaviour.

Socioeconomic Status of the Respondents

This section presents a profile of the sample electorate

based on their socioeconomic background. The following socioeconomic factors are selected to highlight some of the characteristics that are considered relevant for a study of this kind. They are age, educational qualification, marital status, occupational status, and place of residence. The income variable is not included, because the number of response was too small to allow firm conclusions to be drawn.

Table 3.1 show the segment wise size of the sample respondents in each survey area and the number of respondents who were actually interviewed.

Table 3.1
Number of Sample Respondents and Completed Interview

Survey area	*No. of sample respondents*	*No. of completed interviews*
Kohima	42	38
Thizama	48	44
Dimapur	37	34
Ghaspani	53	39
Mokokchung	39	35
Ungma	50	46
Tuensang	41	32
Chare	46	36
Total	356	304

The total number of sample respondents is 356 and the total number of completed interview 304. Therefore, the size of the sample on which survey result is based is 304 and the level of response is 85.39 per cent. Information regarding general background of the respondents was elicited, which allowed the writer to place their voting behaviour within the context of broader socioeconomic factors. The sample electorates were classified in terms of their age, education qualification, marital status, occupation status, and place of residence i.e., (urban-rural).

Distribution of respondents by age

The respondents were divided into four age groups of (i) 18-29, (ii) 30-44, (iii) 45-59, and (iv) 60 and above. The maximum representation in the sample was for the age group of 30–44 with 31 per cent. They were followed by those in the age group of 18–29 with 30 per cent. Those in the age category of 45–59 were represented by 28 per cent. The 60 and above age group are constituted by 11 per cent of the total sample. This is illustrated by Fig 3.1 below.

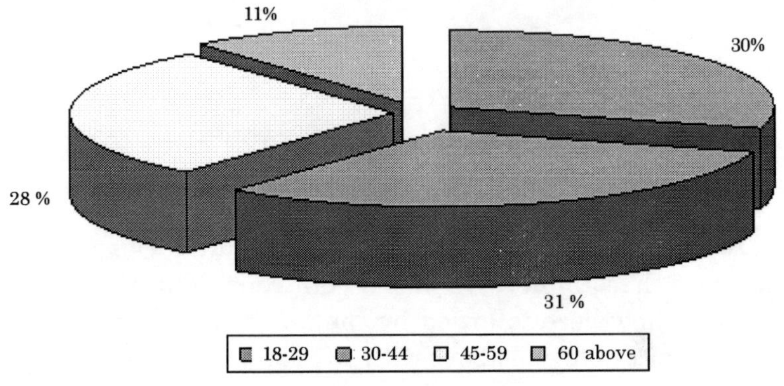

Fig 3.1. Sample Respondents by Age

Distribution of respondents by educational qualification

The education variable is also categorical. Education is measured by the respondent's highest level of educational attainment. The respondents are divided into four categories, measuring their respective level of education, (i) illiterate, (ii) non-metric, (iii) under-graduate, and (iv) graduate and above. Respondents in the illiterate category are those who cannot read or write. Under non-metric group are respondents who have studied in formal school, but have not completed class X. The respondents who are pursuing higher secondary and undergraduate courses come under the group of undergraduate. Women respondents who have completed M.A and pursuing further studies are placed in the graduate and above category.

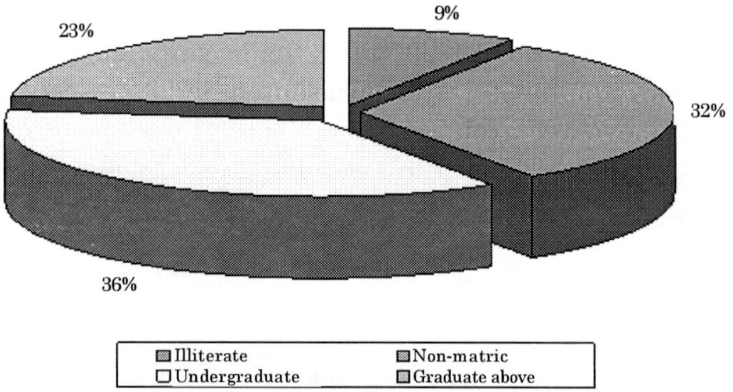

Fig 3.2. Sample Respondents by Educational Qualification

As indicated by Fig.3.2 the undergraduate groupings dominate the sample with 36 per cent representation in the sample. They were followed by the non-matric with 32 per cent, the graduate and above with 23 per cent and the illiterate with 9 per cent representation in the sample.

Distribution of respondents by marital status

Based on marital status, the respondents are classified on the basis of married-unmarried dichotomy. The married respondents clearly dominate the sample with 61 per cent of the total sample, whereas the unmarried respondents are represented with 39 per cent. The reason for the comparatively lower numbers for "unmarried" and higher for "married" respondents in the sample is mainly due to the fact that during interview, especially in the rural areas, many of the respondents in the household were married persons.

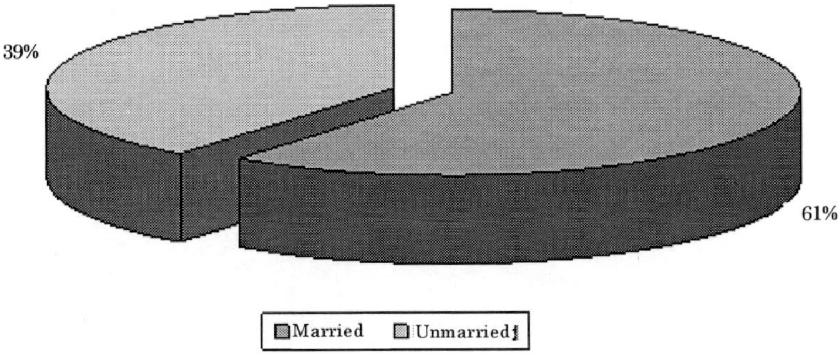

Fig 3.3. Sample Respondents by Marital Status

Distribution of respondents by occupational status

Occupational status is similarly reported as a categorical variable. The respondents are classified into four occupational groups, namely, (i) service, (ii) professionals, (iii) cultivators, and (iv) non-earners. Those in service include both central and state government employees. In the professional category, doctors, lawyers, and school, college and university teachers have been included. In the cultivators category are included the respondents who are engaged in agricultural activities. In the non-earners group students, housewives and those unemployed have been included.

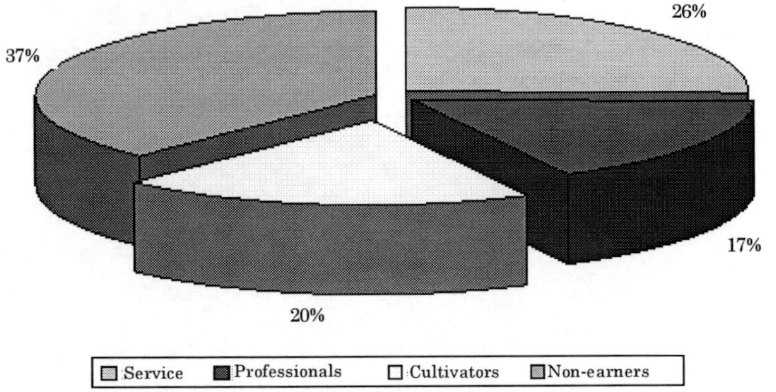

Fig 3.4. Sample Respondents by Occupational Status

Of the sample surveyed, as shown in Fig 3.4, women who are in the paid workforce, 26 per cent of them are in service and 17 per cent come under the professional's category. Those from the cultivator group are represented by 20 per cent. The largest group under the occupational groupings are composed of the non-earners constituting 37 per cent of the sample.

Distribution of respondents by place of residence (urban-rural)

To maintain a comparative perspective, the data concerning the geographical distribution of the respondents are classified according to the type of settlement they live in, ie, their place of residence has been coded as either urban or rural. This allows us to measure whether there is any difference in voting behaviour between the urbanized women voters and their less modern, rural counterparts. The urban respondents constitute 46 per cent of the sample, whereas the rural respondents are represented with 54 per cent in the sample. This is illustrated by Fig 3.5 below.

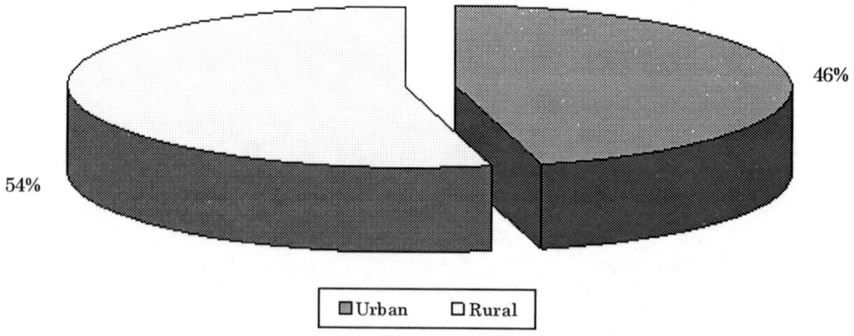

Fig 3.5. Sample Respondents by Place of Residence

The data presented above reveals that a large number of women in the sample are in the age group of 30-44 years

(31%). Many of them are non-earners (37 %). Further, an overwhelming number of women in the sample are married (61%) and 36 per cent of them come under the educational category of undergraduates. Large numbers of women respondents are rural dwellers (54%).

Naga Women's Participation in Voting

Democracy is based on the right of citizens to participate in making the decisions that affect them. This fundamental right finds full meaning only when citizens engage, as actively as possible, in public life. The act of voting is an essential manifestation of that engagement. In fact democratic theory is based on the idea that citizens influence the government through participation in electoral process. It is at the time of election that voters get the opportunity to take part in such activities. It is for this reasons that elections are considered as the cornerstone of democracy.

In this section, an attempt is made to find out the extent of participation by the women voters in voting. The dependent variable is the self-reported turnout, whereas the choice of independent variables are limited to the following items (i) Age, (ii) Educational Qualification, (iii) Occupational Status (iv) Marital Status, and (v) Place of Residence (urban-rural).

The respondent's participation in voting is based on a single question, "Did you vote in the Nagaland Assembly Election of 2008?" with a two-response option -yes or no. Those respondents indicating that they have voted are considered as voters. On the other hand, the sample voters who did not vote are treated as non-voters. As reflected in Fig 3.6, out of 304 respondents who responded, 250 (82 %) of them have exercised their franchise and 54 (18 %) respondents abstained from voting.

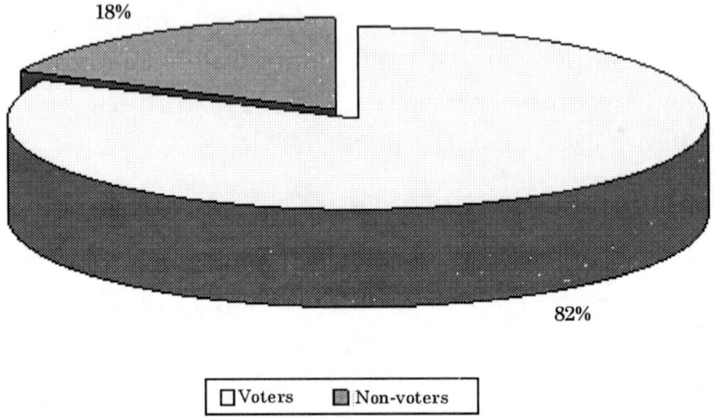

Fig. 3.6. Percentage of Voters and Non-voters

Age and voting

Age is one of the primary criteria for being eligible to vote. For the study, age is measured as a simple proportion of voting age women, who are 18 years and above. Age is considered to have a consistent and significant effect on voter's propensity to vote. Based on the literature survey, older citizens who are in general considered to be more familiar with the political process, are likely to participate in voting more than the younger persons. It means that the young are less likely than the elders to vote.

Despite the fact that 82 per cent of the women in the sample voted, there are large differences in voting participation among the four age groups. It shows that variation in age is strongly associated with turnout at the polls. The study reveals that an increase in age is associated with an increase in reported voting turnout. Voting rises from youth to a peak in the middle age, followed by a slight decline in old age. However, the 60 and above women have voted at a higher rate then women in the 18–29 age category. The most active participants in voting are those women in the age category of 30-59. They voted in large numbers as compared to the younger and the older voters.

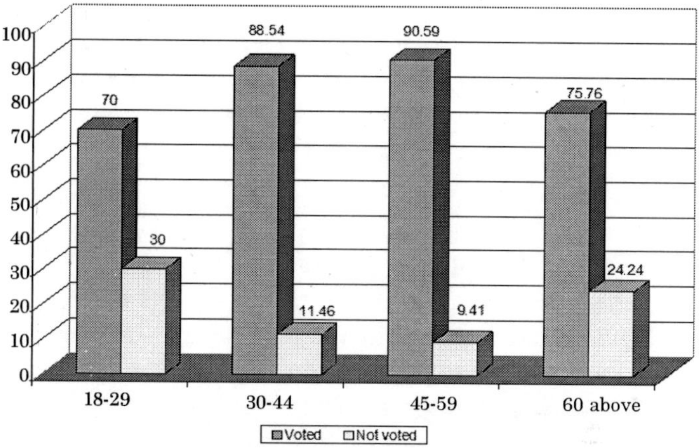

Fig 3.7. Percentage of Voters by Age

Figure 3.7 show that though turnout among women below 30 years of age is not low; they constitute low voting participants in the study. They recorded a voting rate of 70 per cent. Voting turnout continue to grow as age advances, with those in the 30-44 and 45-59 age groups voting in large numbers. They recorded 88.54 per cent and 90.59 per cent voting participation respectively. Voting frequency declines from the 60 and above age groups, but the decline is not much. The elderly tended to take a keener interest to vote than those in the 18-29 age groups. They recorded 75.76 per cent of voting participation.

It is not unusual to find lower turnout among the younger voters. Such patterns are well documented in the literature survey on non-voting. There are several possible reasons why younger voters are not as likely to go to the polls as their older counter parts. They may not be interested in politics. For instance, political issues, parties, and candidates may not be so appealing or important for the younger generation. For them politics may have little relevance because they might be occupied with their education and search for permanent employment.

The positive relationship between advancing age and high voting turnout may be interpreted in different ways. For instance, as people grow older they acquire many resources that promote political participation. Such resources may be in the form of experience, knowledge, skills, and social connections. Many of these resources are considered to motivate people to participate in the electoral process.

As people grow older, they may also start to take an interest in political activities. This is mainly due to the fact that, at this stage people commonly start to settle with families and develop social connections in their local communities. These broader concerns and needs of daily life's may to a considerable extent depend on governmental policies, and this may tend to stimulate participation in political activity. As for those in the 60 and above age group, many people would be entering retirement. Many of them may lose some of their physical mobility necessary to record their vote or getting out to local meetings or political events.

Educational qualification and voting

Education is, in the comparative literature on voting behavior, often deemed the most important predictor of voting behaviour. An extensive, empirical literature in political science has documented a strong correlation between educational attainment and the propensity to vote: the higher the educational qualification of a voter, the higher his or her probability to participate at the polls. There are strong links between the amount of schooling a person has, and the likelihood they will be politically engaged and choose to undertake some type of political participation.[1]

The educated person is a different kind of political actor than the person who has only a little education or none at all.* Gabriel Almond and Sidney Verba hold: "the educaded classes are more likely to be aware of politics (to be aware of the impact of government, to have information about government, to follow politics in the various media)...the more highly educated are also more likely to consider themselves competent to influence the government and free to engage in political discussion.**

*Milbrath, L.W. and Goel, M.L., Political Participation (Chicago: Rand Menally, 1965).
**Almond, G., and S. I. Verba (1963), The Civic Culture: Political Attitudes and Democracy in Five Nations. Primeton Universitgy Press, New Jersey.

There are several possible reasons for such an explanation. The educated are likely to be aware of politics; to have political opinions on a range of subjects; and to engage in political discussions. The more highly educated are also more likely to consider themselves competent to influence the government and be free to engage in political discussions. This set of orientations, widely distributed among those with high education and much less widely distributed among those with low education, constitutes what one might consider the minimum requirements for political participation.[2]

However, the association between educational status and voting raises an interesting paradox in the study. Mention may be made here that the level of literacy for the Naga women has increased overtime (61.46 %).[3] Theoretically, the latter trend should have produced an increase in voting participation among the more literate women. Yet, the study observes precisely the opposite trend. The conventional claim that educational attainment is a critical determinant of voting has not been sustained in the present work. As indicated by Figure 3.8 voting figures does not necessarily raise with a rise the level of education.

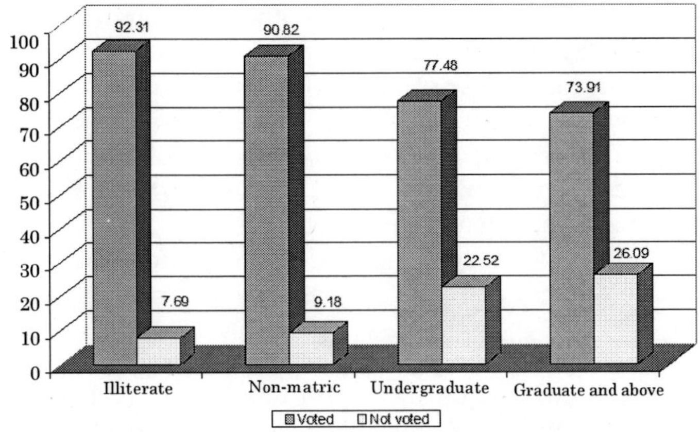

Fig 3.8. Percentage of Voters by Educational Qualification

The illiterate and the nonmatric groups outscore the under-graduate and the graduate and above groups in voting. The illiterate group recorded a voting rate of 92.31 per cent, whereas the non-matric group recorded 90.82 per cent of vote. The under-graduate and the graduate and above groups have lower turnout than those with a few years of schooling (non-matric) and in some cases, those with no schooling at all (illiterate). The undergraduate recorded a voting rate of 77.48 per cent and the graduate and above 73.91 per cent of vote. This is somewhat surprising, as we might expect that a rise in educational level should have led to a higher turnout among the higher educational groups.

The overall picture from the study is that, education does not appear to be a pre-condition for voting because in the category of illiterates and the non-metric the turnout has been high. This finding is also supported by a survey made by Richard Topf. He surveyed data from sixteen European countries in six periods since 1960 and found several instances in which the least educated groups actually have slightly higher turnouts than the most highly educated – contrary to the expected pattern and concludes that there is "no generalized education effect for voting".[4]

No generalization can be made about the apathy of the women voters in the higher educational grouping in Nagaland, unless other studies also confirm this trend. It may however be assumed that voters in these two groups being more educated, may be more aware of the political environment that exists in Nagaland, which is often characterized as corrupt and dirty. Such a trend may be alienating them from the electoral process and as such may have reduced any desire to express a preference by voting.

Occupational status and voting

Occupational status has been conceptually linked to political participation. Women who are not employed are more likely to be non-voters than who are in the paid workforce. Being employed is sometimes taken as a resource that facilitates political participation and is also believed to encourage the development of political attitudes. This is attributed to many reasons. Though voting is an individual act, the social networks in which voting and participation take place are usually the result of social groups. Women's participation in the paid work force outside the home probably lead to wider social and political contacts. They get social opportunities to mix with co-workers and friends, all of which may encourage social and political engagement. Further, women who are employed could be exposed to politics-oriented influence of their colleagues. For instance, they might get opportunity to discuss political matters with others.

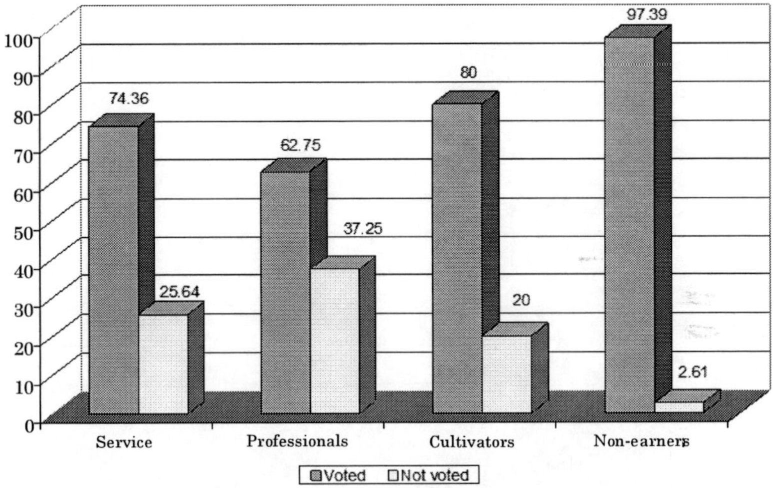

Fig 3.9. Percentage of Voters by Occupational Status

The result in figure 3.9 however shows mixed results. No clear picture of any significant relation between women's occupation and turnout emerges. The non-earners recorded the highest voting turnout (97.39 %). The cultivators who are mostly illiterate with a low-income level have recorded a high turnout of 80 per cent. They were followed by those women in service with a voting rate of 74.36 per cent. The professionals turned up for voting in lesser numbers. They recorded a turnout of 62.75 per cent. Such differences in turnout levels among different occupational groups appear to be influenced more by their level educational attainment than by this occupation.

Marital status and voting

There is a general observation in the literature on political participation that married women vote more often than the unmarried women. By examining the association of the marital status variable on voting, an attempt has been made to assess the importance of the married and unmarried status, if any, on women voting participation.

Figure 3.10 show that 86.96 per cent of married respondents reported voting as compared to 75 per cent of unmarried respondents. It is evident that married women are much more likely to exercise their franchise than the unmarried women.

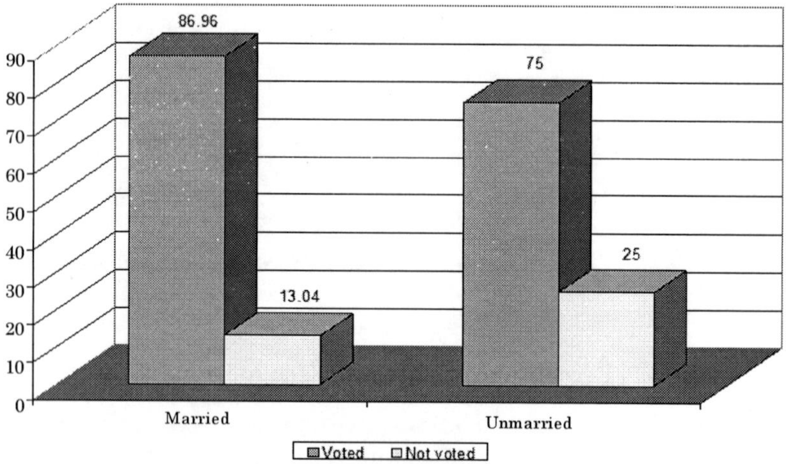

Fig 3.10. Percentage of Voting by Marital Status

The reason why the married women turn out at the polls in considerably larger numbers than the unmarried women could be attributed to several reasons. It may be possible that the married women are persuaded by their husbands to vote for the candidate of their choice. Husband and wife voting as units, might therefore be attributed as to why voting turnout among the married respondents is high. Studies of patterns of within household variation of voting in some countries have produced extremely powerful evidence in support of the general contention that people who live together vote together and also change their minds together between elections.[5]

Place of residence and voting

For a basis of comparability, women from urban and rural units have been taken for the present study. When we examine the data as displayed in figure 3.11, the result reveals that the rural respondents are more active than the urban respondents as far as voting participation is concerned. The rural voters recorded a turnout of 85.63 per cent, whereas the urban respondents recorded 78.10 per cent of vote.

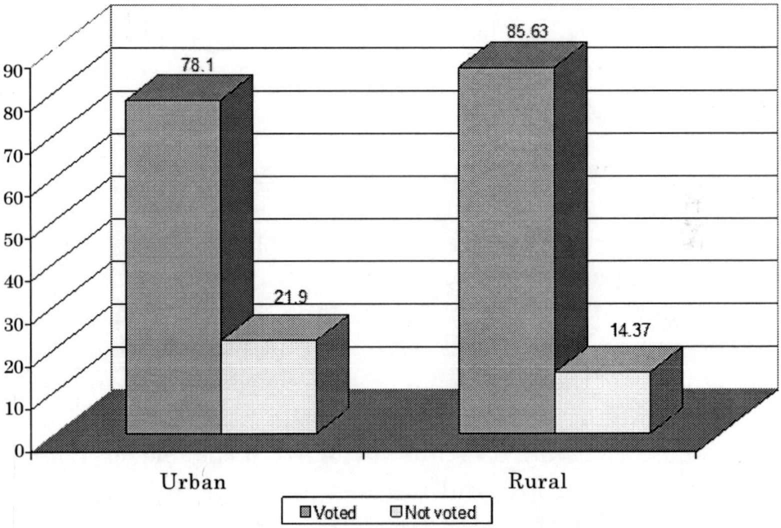

Fig 3.11. Percentage of Voting by Place of Residence

One way of interpreting the data as highlighted above is that, in Nagaland more than half of the population (82.77 %) live in the rural areas.[6] In other words, in Nagaland majority of the votes come from the rural areas. This factor, generally lead to large scale mobilization efforts by the candidates and political parties especially in the rural areas. This could be one of the reasons why turnout in Nagaland among the rural electorate is usually high across genders.

Another explanation could be that, in Nagaland, economy of the rural areas is mainly based on agriculture and related activities. A large number of the women respondents from rural areas belong to the farming households. Resource scarcity may increase the impact of party efforts to buy votes, which is a common occurrence in Nagaland. Vote buying may consists in many cases of simple gifts, patronage, and exchange of money. Restated, voters in the rural areas may be more susceptible to the promises of patronage from political parties and candidates due to their precarious economic situation. Some of them may vote in exchange for material goods or money and some in the hope that their vote may affect some changes.

Reasons for Voting

Voters cast their vote for various reasons. Some people feel pride for the effort put into being informed and involved. Others vote out of a sense of duty because of their belief in democratic participation. It is also possible that some voters base their vote wholly or in part, on other criteria, such as under the influence of the male household members, the personality of the party leaders, the record or performance of the incumbent government and the state of their own economic well being. It is thus obvious that the reasons behind the act of voting are multifarious. In order to find out the reasons, which motivate the women voters to vote and whether they exercise their franchise independently, they were asked the reasons for casting their vote.

The respondent's reasons for voting, as given in figure 3.12, were based on the responses given to an open-ended question, "what is the reason/s to vote for a particular candidate of a particular party?" The open-ended question allowed the respondent to answer in their own words. In this way, the writer was able to explore more fully some of the attitudes and feelings that lie behind the reason for voting among women and whether they exercise their voting independently.

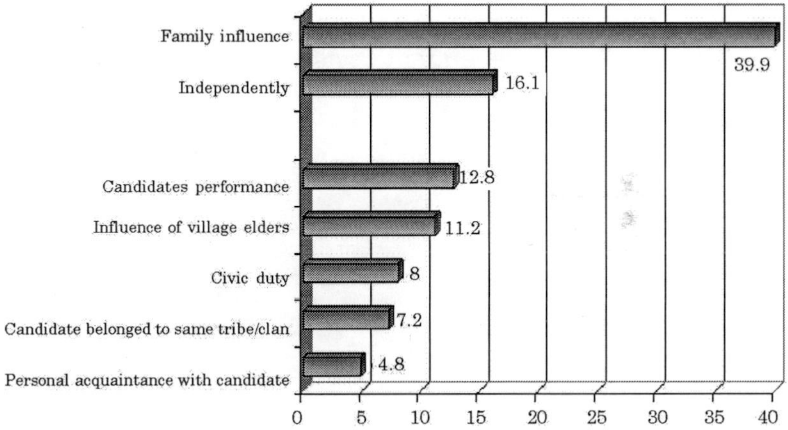

Fig 3.12. Reasons for Voting in Assembly Election, 2008

It appears that majority of the respondents deemed discussion among the family members as very influential in determining their vote. This reason stands as the most important reason for the majority of the women voters to vote. As summarized in figure 3.12, 39.2 per cent of the respondents voted at the behest of family influence. One respondent asserted the fact that, family should not be divided on its choice of party/candidate.[7] Whereas, another respondent, who exercised her voting choice independently argues that women have a right to choose their own party or candidate.[8]

It thus appears that though some women tend to take pride in their seemingly autonomy at making electoral choice (16.8 %), majority of them identify the family as an important factor influencing their vote. The reason why women do not vote for a candidate or political party of their choice could be reflective of the gendered power relations within the household. For instance, very few women take part in the family decision making. This is generally taken by the male household members. Just few of them (11 %) take decision in the household as shown in Fig 3.13. The existence of gendered power relations at home level may affect women's sense of freedom to make independent decisions in other areas also.

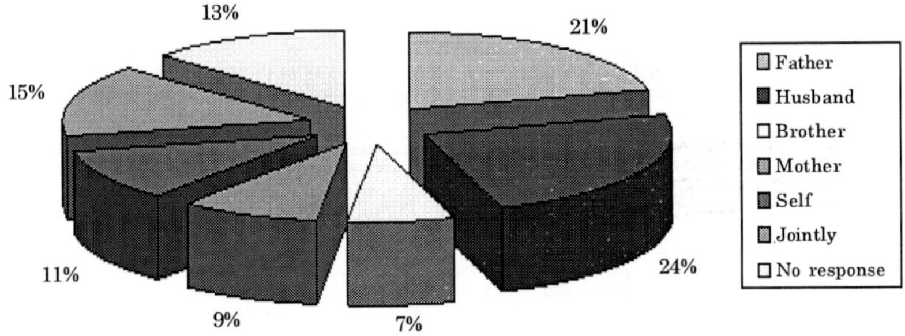

Fig 3.13. Decision-making Pattern at Home

For 12.8 per cent of the respondent, candidate's performance was the underlying reason for their voting choice. This reason was followed by 11.2 per cent of respondents who voted because the elders of their village convinced them to vote for a particular candidate or party. In a typical village election scenario, in many villages in Nagaland, pre-arranged agreement is made between political parties and the village elders. The latter then try to convince the villagers to vote for that party or candidate. This is how patronage relationship is produced. Village elders who are known to influence the opinion of many others may be specially favored and may be given benefits if the candidate is successful.

Civic duty was the basis of voting for 8 per cent of the respondents. Another 7.2 per cent asserted that they voted because the candidate belonged to their tribe/clan. Personal acquaintance with the candidate was the reason given by 4.8 per cent of the sample voters.

Reasons for not voting

Those reported not having voted, were asked to give their reasons for not voting. They were asked an open-ended question, "If you did not vote, what is the main reason/s for not voting?" The study found that the non-voters are disproportionately young, unmarried, educated, professionals and urban residents. Behind the superficial reasons given for not voting, like being out of station (5.56 %), busy (5.56 %) and sick (3.7 %), majority of those who did not register to vote explained their reasons by a skeptical attitude towards the political party or candidate, elections and their consequences.

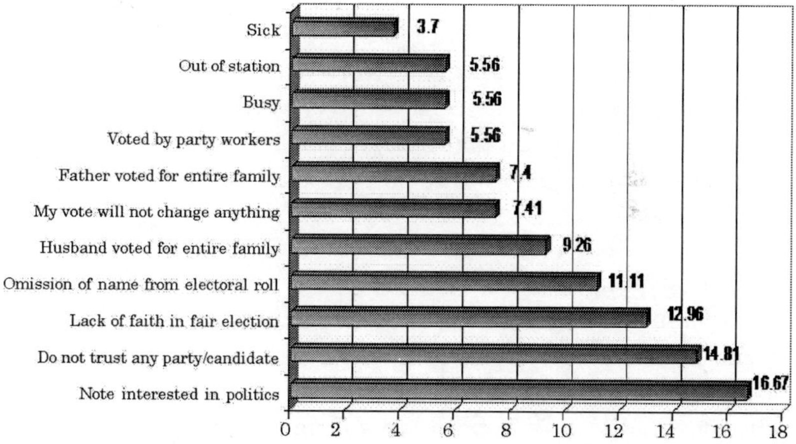

Fig 3.14. Reasons for Not Voting in the Assembly Election, 2008

As reported in Fig 3.14, amongst the diverse responses given by the collective of non-voters, lack of interest in politics (16.67%) was the largest single group of responses given for not voting. This reason was followed by respondents (14.81%) who cited that they did not vote because they do not trust any party or candidate. Another 12.96 per cent of the respondents cited lack of faith in fair election, as the reason for not voting. Some (11.11 %) cited omission of name in the electoral roll, as the reason for not voting. 9.26 per cent of the respondents could not exercise their franchise because their husbands voted for the entire family. 7.40 per cent did not vote as their father voted for them. While 7.41 per cent of the respondents said there was no point in voting because their vote will not change anything, another 5.56 per cent of them did not vote because the party workers had voted for them.

From the above analysis it seems apparent that women voters do not exercise their franchise independently. Majority of them voted under the influence of family members. In this context, it is pertinent to mention that while democracy generally means voluntary political participation, the study finds that many women did not enjoy a free choice in voting for the candidate of their choice. They were deprived of their full right to elect their representative, because their vote was cast either by their husband or the party workers. This goes against the principle of "one person, one vote".

Conclusion

To summarize, the reported turnout of the women respondents is high (82.24 %). Contrary to many studies on turnout, the positive association between different aspects of socio economic status and voting is only partially established. The most active participants in voting are women in the 45-59 age group, the illiterate, the non-earners, the married, and the rural respondents. Whereas, among the less active voting participants, are women in the 18-29 age group, those having the highest educational qualification, women professionals, the unmarried and women residing in the urban areas.

Though some of the women tend to take pride in their autonomy at making electoral choice, the study found that majority of the women identifies the family as an important factor in determining their voting choice. Among the non-voters, majority cited lack of interest in politics as the reason for not exercising their franchise.

NOTES

1. Sidney Verba, *et al.* (1993), "Citizens Activity: Who Participate? What Do They Say?" *American Political Science Review*, Vol.87, No.2, pp.303-318.

2. G. Almond and S. Verba (1963), *The Civic Culture: Political Attitudes and Democracy in Five Nations.* Princeton University Press, New Jersey, pp.318-19.

3. *Statistical Handbook of Nagaland*, Government of Nagaland, 2001.

4. Topf, R. (1995), 'Electoral Participation', in Hans-Dieter Klingemann and Deiter Fuchs, (eds) *Citizens and the State*, Oxford University Press, Oxford.

5. Johnston, R. *et al.*, "A Missing Level in the analysis of British Voting Behavior: The household as Context as Shown by Analysis of a 1992-1997 Longitudinal Survey." ESRC Research Methods Programme, *Working Paper No 3.*, September 2003

6. *Statistical Handbook of Nagaland*, Government of Nagaland, 2001.

7. Respondent.

8. Respondent.

4

Participation of Women in Electoral Activities

Introduction

Voting is one very good indicator of people's participation in the electoral process. However, in the context of women, even if voting turnout is high it may not necessarily mean a high level of political participation. Voting is an activity in which even the least involved women can participate. Moreover, voting has its own strength and weakness as a tool of political participation, especially in the context of women. Its strength is in its capacity to increase political equality. Millions of women can be observed in the political process only through voting. It has a powerful equalizing and mobilizing effect on them. Still the act of voting by itself is not able to generate political equality.[1]

Therefore, in order to analyze voting behaviour of women in its entirety, there is a need to go beyond the act of voting, and try to look at women's participation in other modes of political activities as well. Voting is no doubt one of the most traditional and basic forms of political participation in a representative democracy. However, a genuinely participatory political culture involves far more than simply the periodic casting of votes. Compared with voting, a greater intensity of participation is possible. Some of these activities are campaign activities, party membership, and political discussion. These are electoral activities that take place not just at the time of election but also in between elections. These forms of electoral activities may offer greater opportunity for personal influence or involvement.

The analysis in the previous chapter (Chapter III) reveals that women voters tend to vote in large numbers. However, we do not know whether they carry this enthusiasm over to other forms of electoral activities. Voting turnout can often overstate the extent to which the citizens can truly participate in public decision-making. This is because voting figures cannot be relied upon to provide a clear indication of women's participation in other forms of electoral activities. This necessitates an examination on women participation in other modes of electoral activities.

Modes of Electoral Participation

In different democracies people's participation in politics has taken a variety of forms, and this has gradually extended the scope of electoral politics beyond voting. Political scientists have categorized different modes of electoral activities by which people can participate in politics. These include (i) running for or holding public or party office, (ii) belonging to a party or other political organization, (iii) working in an election, (iv) attending political meetings or rallies, (v) making financial contribution to a party or a candidate, (vi) contacting a public official, (vii) publicly expressing a political opinion to convince others, (viii) participating in political discussion, (ix) voting, and (x) exposing oneself to political stimuli.[2]

For the present chapter, the following forms of electoral activities have been included as indices to measure the degree of participation in electoral activities. Voting is not included as it has been studied in detail in chapter III.

- Campaigning for a candidate or political party
- Attending election meetings
- Membership in political party
- Taking part in political discussion.

The term election campaign is used to describe the persuasive activities that go on in the period before the actual casting of votes. There are many types of campaign activities like campaigning or canvassing for a candidate or party, making financial contribution, collecting funds, distributing pamphlets, etc. A campaign activity is typified in this study by campaigning for a candidate or party and attending party meetings. Campaign activities require a lot of mobility, time, and initiative on the part of the participant. In Nagaland, women campaigners are usually seen canvassing door to door, soliciting the votes of the general electorate. The political parties also deploy their women campaigners to mobilize the women voters.

Attending election meeting or rallies is another mode of electoral participation. Election meetings are usually organized by various political parties and people attend these meetings to express their solidarity in favor of a candidate and a political party, and also to listen to what the leaders have to say in the meetings. By attending election meeting the voter can get a lot of information, beyond who is running for what office. Informed voters can make good use of their vote and they may have more awareness of the election issues and the candidates. Besides, attending election meetings may also motivate the voters to take part in other forms of electoral activities.

Membership in political party is another mode of electoral participation. Political parties provide ways for citizens to participate in politics. People become members of a political party for different reasons. For many people political party may be the most common channel for gaining political experience. They provide an opportunity for involvement in public affairs. Some may join a party for personal interest, some under the influence of family members or friends; still some may become members of party with a commitment that they may be able to do something for the community. Whatever may be the reasons for joining a political party, being a member is likely to generate an interest to take part in electoral activities.

Discussing politics with others constitute another mode of electoral participation. The literature survey shows that discussing politics and current events with others motivate a person to become more active in political activities. Through discussion the participant is able to know the elements of politics and arrive at some understanding of the political issues. People generally discuss and talk about issues of concern with each other. One who discusses public affairs with others may increase his or her knowledge and information needed to evaluate candidates and issues intelligently. This awareness in turn may induce the person to participate in electoral activities. Willingness to engage in political discussion implies an active orientation to politics. By discussing political issues with others, people may become quiet political minded. Further, the experience of discussing public affairs with others may also stimulate a sense of political engagement.

Naga Women's Participation in Electoral Activities

A number of variables that the literature survey has established as important correlates of citizen's participation in politics have been employed. These variables include age, education, occupation, marital status and place of residence. These variables help to capture the effects of the standard predictors of citizen's participation in electoral activities besides voting. The main dependent variable is whether or not the respondents participated in other forms of electoral activities.

For measuring participation in campaign activity the respondents were asked whether they had campaigned for any candidate or party during the State Assembly Election held in 2008. Similarly they were asked whether they had attended any of the election meetings organized during the election campaign. For measuring party membership, the respondents were asked whether they are a member of any political party, with a two-response answer-yes or no. For measuring political discussion, frequency—frequently, sometimes, and never—of discussing politics and public affairs with family members, friends, neighbours, and acquaintances have been included.

Electoral participation and age

Table 4.1 reports the participation level of the four age groups in various forms of electoral activities. Taking data from campaigned for candidate column, women in the age group of 45-59 years appear to be the most active participants as campaigners (43.24 %), followed by women in the 30-44 age group (37.84 %) and18-29 age category (18.92 %). None from the 60 and above group campaigned for a candidate.

Table 4.1
Participation in Electoral Activities by Age

Age	*Electoral Activities*			*Political discussion*		
	Campaigned for candidate	*Attended election meetings*	*Party member-ship*	*F*	*S*	*N*
18-29	18.92	12.94	22.64	26.67	43.33	30
30-44	37.84	30.59	28.30	31.25	46.88	21.87
45-59	43.24	38.82	33.97	37.65	47.06	15.29
60 and Above	0	17.65	15.09	30.30	45.45	24.25

*F-frequently; S-sometimes; N-never

When it comes to attending election meetings, it is again the women in 45-59 age group (38.82 %) who reported a higher propensity to attend election meetings. They were followed by women in the age group of 30-44 (30.59 %). The 60 and above women (17.65%) appear to be more inclined to attend election meetings than the younger respondents in the 18-29 age group (12.94 %).

Similarly, the 45–59 age group dominates the sample when it comes to membership in political party. Among them, 33.97 per cent are members of some political party. In the 30-44 age group 28.30 per cent reported being members of a political party. The younger respondents reported 22.64 per cent membership in a political party. Just 15.09 per cent of the 60 and above respondents are members of political party.

The data dealing with political discussion similarly reveals women in the 45–59 years (37.65 %) as being more inclined to discuss politics frequently with others. They were followed by women in the 30–44 age group, with 31.25 per cent of them engaging in political discussion frequently. Women who are 60 and above (30.30 %) show higher interest in discussing politics than the younger women in the 18-29 age group (26.67 %). The data indicate that women who discuss politics more frequently are also the most active participants in all modes of electoral activities including voting. It thus appears that women in the 45-59 age groups appear to be most active in all the indicators of electoral activities.

Thus, the above data reveals that, 45-59 years period is the time when most women actively engage in politics. During this period women are comparatively free from biological responsibility. Moreover, being mature, they gain a lot of experience, including political experience. As for the younger women, one of the reasons why their participation rate is low could be their indifference and lack of interest in politics. This in turn could be because most of them would be spending much of their time in pursuit of their education and careers. Another factor could be due to the reason that, electoral activities presuppose public roles and a lot of visibility. In a patriarchal society like Nagaland, there are invisible, yet strong social prescriptions against female participation in politics. Most of the young voters are likely to be unmarried. There would be many questions around her moral standing if she actively engages in electoral activities. These are some of the reasons, which have held down young women's participation in electoral activities.

The older women (60 and above) as compared with the 18-29 age group show greater interest in attending election meetings as well as greater inclination to discuss politics frequently. However, their participation in campaigning was the lowest among all the age categories. Campaigning for a candidate is an activity that entails a lot of mobility, energy and time. Advanced age may reduce the opportunities for being active in this type of activity because the range of feasible activities becomes more restricted as one gets older.

Electoral participation and educational qualification

Table 4.2 in the following page reports electoral participation of women from the four educational groups. Certain electoral activities, such as, campaigning, attending election meetings and party membership are not dependent on women's level of education. For these modes of electoral activities, women with no education (illiterate) or moderate education (Non-matric) are the most active whereas the least active participants are women having the highest education qualification (graduate and above).

Therefore, as educational level goes up, participation in campaigning, attending election meetings and party membership comes down. There may be several reasons as to why the more educated women do not participate in these modes of electoral activities. The nature of politics that exists in Nagaland may be an important reason. In Nagaland like in any other states in India, instance of large scale electoral corruption and malpractice is very common. Violence at the polling centers is also a regular feature. Such practices give a bad reputation to politics. Women who involve in these activities get a bad reputation. This reduces the enthusiasm of women, especially the more educated, from involvement in electoral activities, leading to their low level of electoral participation.

Table 4.2
Participation in Electoral Activities by Educational Qualification

Educational status	*Electoral Activities*			*Political discussion*		
	Campaigned for candidate	*Attended election meetings*	*Party membership*	*F*	*S*	*N*
Illiterate	40.54	38.82	41.52	7.69	15.39	76.92
Non-Matric	29.73	29.42	28.30	34.70	28.57	36.73
UG	18.92	20	20.75	53.15	35.14	11.71
G and Above	10.81	11.76	9.43	63.77	36.23	0

* F-frequently; S- sometimes; N- never; UG-under graduate; G-graduate

On the other hand, participation in campaigning, election meeting, and party membership has been relatively high from the lower educational groups. It is possible that the illiterate, those with less education (non-matric), and also those who are in college are more likely to be susceptible to the lure of money. Moreover, many of them are also likely to be unemployed. Some of them may engage in the above-cited electoral activities in exchange for monetary gain.

The picture is however changed when we examine the data on political discussion. The data reveals that education is strongly related to engagement in political discussion. For example, the frequency of political discussion rises with a rise in the level of educational attainment. Those who discuss politics more frequently came from women having the highest educational status, the graduate and above (63.77 %). They were followed by the undergraduates (53.15 %). Among the non-metric 34.70 per cent of them, discuss politics frequently, while those who have no education at all discuss politics less frequently (7.69 %).

The reason why the more educated tend to discuss politics more frequently is not far to seek. To engage in political discussion, one generally needs to have knowledge about a lot of issues. The educated may be more aware of a wide range of issues. This may be one of the reasons why they tend to engage in political discussion with other people more frequently. But they do not carry over this interest to the more public form of electoral activities such as campaign activities, election meetings and party membership.

The above data shows that education has different impact on different modes of electoral activities. For instance, education and involvement in electoral activities does not hold for such activities as campaigning for a candidate or party, attending election meetings and party membership, except for political discussion.

Electoral participation and occupational status

It is generally held that those who are gainfully employed are most likely to participate in electoral activities than those who are unemployed. However, the relation between women's occupational status and their participation in different modes of electoral activities is only partially supported, as indicated in Table 4.3.

The result indicate that women professionals and those in service are less involved in the more public forms of electoral activities, such as, campaigning for candidate, attending election meetings and party membership. Their participation tends to confine more to political discussion. Reading data from campaigned for candidate column; the non-earners (40.54 %) are the most active, closely followed by the cultivators (35.14 %). Women who are in service (13.51 %) and the professionals (10.81 %) appear to be least interested in campaigning for election candidates.

Table 4.3
Participation in Electoral Activities by Occupational Status

Occupational status	*Electoral Activities*			*Political discussion*		
	Campaigned for candidate	*Attended election meetings*	*Party membership*	*F*	*S*	*N*
Service	13.51	11.76	18.87	35.90	41.03	23.07
Professionals	10.81	9.41	13.21	43.14	39.22	17.64
Cultivators	35.14	37.65	30.18	23.33	30	46.67
Non-earners	40.54	41.18	37.74	21.74	40	38.26

*F-frequently; S-sometimes; N-never.

The data on attending election meetings show a similar pattern, with the non-earners (41.18 %) and cultivators (37.65 %) showing more enthusiasm, than women who are in service (11.76 %) and the professionals (9.41).

As for party membership, 37.74 per cent of women from the non-earners category are members of a political party. They are closely followed by the cultivators with 30.18 per cent of them affiliated to a political party. Unlike women from these two occupational groups, 18.87 per cent of women in service and 13.21 per cent of women professionals are members of a party.

The study finds that, among all the occupational groups, women professionals and those in service are least active in campaigning for candidate, attending meetings and party membership. Their low participation could be accounted for by their level of education. The professionals usually have higher level of education. The analysis in the previous page has indicated low participation rate by the more educated. Maybe due to the negative character associated with politics, the more educated generally hesitate from participating in the more public political activities.

However, the professionals (43.14 %) and those in service (35.90 %) dominate the sample when it comes to discussing politics frequently. Unlike high rate of participation in campaigning, election meetings and party membership, the participation rate of the non-earners and the cultivators tends to slide down when it comes to political discussion. Around 23.33 per cent of cultivators and 21.74 per cent among the non-earners engage in political discussion frequently.

Electoral participation and marital status

The literature review indicates that married persons participate at a higher rate than those who are not married across numerous electoral activities. Table 4.4 indicates the relationship between marital status on the one hand and participation in electoral activities on the other. The married respondents (64.86 %) appear be have campaigned for party candidate at a higher rate than the unmarried respondents (35.14 %). This shows that the married respondents take an active part in campaigning than the unmarried women.

Regarding participation in election meetings, 57.65 per cent of the married respondents and 42.33 per cent of unmarried respondents reported attending election meeting. Being members of some political party is also dependent on the marital status of the women voters. Just 43.39 per cent of the unmarried respondents are members of political party as compared to 56.61 per cent of the married respondents. This shows that majority of the married respondents as compared to the unmarried respondents are affiliated to one party or the other. Similarly, the married respondents (25.54 %) discuss politics more frequently than those who are not married (22.5 %).

Table 4.4
Participation in Electoral Activities by Marital Status

Marital status	*Electoral Activities*			*Political discussion*		
	Campaigned for candidate	*Attended election meetings*	*Party member-ship*	*F*	*S*	*N*
Married	64.86	57.65	56.61	25.54	49.46	25
Unmarried	35.14	42.35	43.39	22.5	40.83	36.67

*F-frequently; S-sometimes; N-never.

The data show that the unmarried respondents as compared to the married respondents are only minimally engaged in all the indicators of electoral activities. This means that many of the unmarried respondents demonstrate behaviour that by most standard falls short of what it takes to be an engaged citizen. For an unmarried woman there may be lot of problem participating in electoral activities. For instance, by and large, women who actively take part in electoral activities are viewed with suspicion and are generally subjected to a lot of gossip and speculation as regards her character. Whereas men are comparatively free from such public scrutiny. For an unmarried woman, the risk factor of involving in politics is more because involvement in politics may compromise her feminity by way of question on her moral character and this could hurt her marriage chances. These may be some of the possible reasons why participation by unmarried respondents has been low in all the indices of electoral activities as compared to the married respondents.

Electoral participation and place of residence

The urban-rural difference in electoral participation is

reported in Table 4.5. The data shows that place of residence have different effect on different categories of electoral activities. The rural respondents (59.46 %) are more active in campaigning for a candidate than the urban dwellers (40.54 %). The same trend is reflected when it comes to data on attending election meetings. The rural respondents (60 %) are more inclined to attend meeting than the urban (40 %) respondents

Table 4.5
Participation in Electoral Activities by Place of Residence

Place of residence	*Electoral Activities*			*Political discussion*		
	Campaigned for candidate	*Attended election meetings*	*Party member-ship*	*F*	*S*	*N*
Urban	40.54	40	37.74	26.95	44.91	28.14
Rural	59.46	60	62.26	21.17	42.34	36.49

*F-frequently; S-sometimes; N-never.

Data on party membership reveal a similar result. 62.26 per cent of the rural respondents are members of some political party as compared to 37.74 per cent of the urban respondents. However, the urban respondents (26.95 %) show more inclination to discuss politics more frequently than the rural respondents (21.17 %).

In examining the data, the result shows that in most indicators of electoral activities, the urban dwellers are less active than the rural dwellers. This seems to be quite surprising because the urban residents are more exposed to the channels of modernizations like the mass media, better education, etc. All these factors are believed to be significantly related to political participation. Their electoral participation appears to confine more to discussing politics.

Several reasons may be accounted for why women from rural areas are more active by way of participation in electoral activities. Political parties and the candidates tend to target the rural electorate more than the urban electorate. This is mainly because around 82.77 per cent of the population in Nagaland reside in rural areas.[3] It means the bulk of the vote in Nagaland comes from the rural electorate. In many villages in Nagaland, at the time of election a preliminary vote takes place to select the candidate/party to be supported by the entire village. This decision is usually taken by the village councils, by virtue of it being the highest decision making body at the village level. The logic behind such electoral practice is mainly economic reasons. The village elders and the candidate/party enter into pre-election bargain, whereby the village elders persuade the entire village to support the candidate/party in return for community favors in terms of certain economic gain. This results in high rate of participation across gender in the rural areas.

Sometimes, within a village, people are divided into factions, supporting candidates of different political parties. Each faction mobilizes themselves and work together to see that their candidate wins. In the process, the electorate both men and women are mobilized to participate in different modes of electoral activities. This could possibly be another reason why women from rural areas are more active in electoral activities.

The summarization of women's participation in different modes of electoral activities is highlighted by Table 4.6 below.

Table 4.6
Overall Participation of Women in Electoral Activities

Electoral activities	*Total number of respondents who participated*
Campaigned for a candidate	12.17 (37)
Attended election meetings	27.96 (85)
Party membership	17.43 (53)

The study reveals that, women voters duly go to the poll to cast their vote (Chapter III), but their electoral participation in other forms of electoral activities, as illustrated by Table 4.6, is just marginal. This shows that women in Nagaland have been able to strengthen their political visibility only as voters. Therefore, the key finding is simply disengagement of women in electoral activities except in voting. There is an apparent desire on the part of some women to become involved in the various indices of electoral activities, but reluctance on the part of some not to do so. Women's participation in voting is high (82.23 %). However, just a minimal number (12.17 %) of them reported campaigning for a candidate or party. This reveals that participation in campaign activity remains very much a minority pursuit for women in Nagaland. Campaigning for a candidate is a public activity. One needs to be physically mobile which necessitates remaining outside the home at places at odd hours. Such activities also demand a significant, inflexible time, and commitment. Compounding this problem there is also the fear of gaining a bad reputation. Women who are involved in politics face seemingly public scrutiny about their character. This is mainly due to the fact that politics in Nagaland has come to have a very negative connotation. It is often labelled as dirty and corrupt. Attending election meeting is moderately high (27.96 %) as compared to taking part in campaigning.

The data indicates that very few women are members of a political party (17.43%). Such findings may pose some significant challenges for the political parties in Nagaland. Women's low membership in political party could possibly mean that the parties have not done enough to mobilize them. Most of the political parties have an instrumentalist outlook towards women's electoral participation. They mobilize women voters just as an electoral force for the purpose of mustering votes for their party's candidates in the election. It could also be possible that, women are not interested to become a member of political party due to the negative image associated with political parties.

The study also found that while very few respondents (24 %) engage in political discussion frequently, 46 per cent of them engage in political discussion sometimes, and 30 per cent of the respondents never discuss politics. This result is illustrated by Fig 4.1.

Discussing politics with others is a matter of interest and awareness. This could imply two things. Either women are not interested in politics or their awareness about politics or related issue is low.

Overall, women in the 45-59 age group, those with no education, non-earners, women who are married, and the rural respondents were found to be the most active in voting, campaigning for a candidate, attending election meetings and party membership. The respondents from the highest educational group appear unwilling to engage in any form of electoral activity aimed at influencing decisions, except for political discussion.

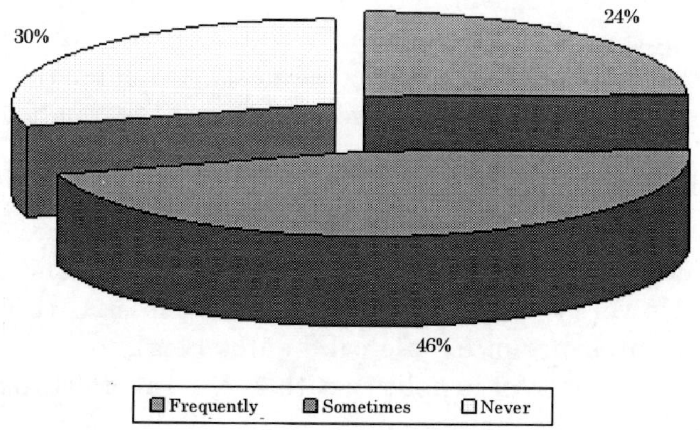

Fig. 4.1. Overall Participation of Women in Political Discussion

Impediments to Women's Participation in Electoral Activities

In surveying the reasons which restrict Naga women's capacity to actively participate in the politicl life, the study notice that these obstacles are multifarious. Some of these are cultural, in a social environment that does not support the idea of women participation in politics and some are self-imposed, in that women simply lack the confidence and interest to engage in politics. Added to these barriers, women are yet to overcome the psychology of subordination, especially in politics. The other impediments are time and economic constraints and the prevariling political environment.

Before beginning a discussion on the obstacles to women's participation, it is useful to mention why women's participation in electoral activities is critical. True democracy is characterized by the full participation of both the gender in all spheres of public life. As women make up nearly half of the population of the state, women's full participation in public affairs should be recognized as a fundamental condition for democracy. As the government is legitimized through people's participation, legitimacy of political institutions will be undermined if sections of the community do not participate. Another reason as to why women's participation in all forms of electoral activities is important is based on the argument that the visible presence of women in the public sphere may motivate other women to participate in the electoral processes. Mention may be made here the result of a study conducted by two University of Notre Dame political scientists. According to them, presence of female candidates heightened female adolescent's interest in politics with long term effects on the political engagement of women.[4]

Theories abound as to why women in general are not drawn to politics as much as men are. In assessing women's minimal participation in electoral activities, one must examine the inter-connections between the socio - cultural values and practices that are firmly entrenched in the systems and structures of society. This is because the culture of the society determines the level of women's participation in the public sphere. In a traditional society like ours, by traditional norms, women are usually expected to stay at home and take up the responsibility for the caring of the family and household needs. It is not uncommon to see Naga woman managing the household work along with her job. This leaves very little time for engagement in other activities.

On the other hand, women's low participation in electoral activities is often explained by the stereotype of their being uninterested in politics. There might be some degree of disinterest among women to take part in electoral activities, but the reality that is often overlooked is that, their struggle to handle dual roles, limits their time and energy for political activities. For many women, with their primary roles as mothers and wives, they are left with little time to engage in electoral activities. In Nagaland, despite major changes in gender roles in recent decades, women are usually expected to take care of the household and related responsibilities and at the same time, for some, to handle a full-time job and a career. As a result, the basic responsibilities and patterns of their lives, with more focus on family, and related responsibilities, make it impossible for them to sustain their electoral participation beyond voting.

The major drawback for many women is that the relationship that exist in the domestic arena, with male household member as the head, is translated to what is generally perceived as the public. This becomes quiet prominent when the subject is politics. Typically political participation is viewed in terms of activities, which takes place in a public arena. For instance, electoral activities such as campaigning for a candidate or party or attending election meetings are all public activity. Such activities are usually assigned for male members of the society. Women on the other hand are assigned specific roles centered around family, children, and private life. Moreover, unlike their male counterparts, women do not receive positive reinforcement from the society for participation in politics, which is generally regarded as a male occupation. This cultural limitation has pushed women to traditional roles, which does not bode well for women's role in the public arena. This is not an uncommon position for Naga women generally.

Therefore, the association of women with the private sphere leads to their total marginalization from political life. It appears that women themselves are aware of such gender specific roles. Some of the women interviewed had explicitly referred to the traditional conceptions of gender roles to explain why they participate less in electoral activities. One of the respondents said:

> "There is a sequence in what we should do as women: we go to school, then get married, have children, get them married and so on".

Another woman expressed a similar view:

> "I feel the women's place is in the home bringing up the children".

These comments highlight the fact that traditional gender role stereotypes are still present in our society, leading women to conceptualize their roles in the political arena differently. It seems clear that the separation between the 'private and the public' spaces is still accepted as a natural division between the genders in Nagaland. Therefore, the societal understanding of what constitutes the private and public space may lie at the heart of some of the difficulties faced by women in taking part in electoral activities.

Some of the women interviewed reflected their psychological barrier to participation in electoral activities.

The reasons for this can be traced both historically and contemporaneously. One of the reasons could be the historical exclusion of women from politics and political leadership. Men's dominance of leadership in almost all institutions of power may be sending a message that only men can take part in the electoral process. This entrenched belief that politics is inherently a masculine domain has impacted negatively on women's involvement in electoral politics.

Gender disparity in politics is still a problem in Nagaland. Much commentary on electoral participation assumes that, if women believe that gender equality in politics have not yet been achieved; they might not be motivated to take part in the political process. However, it is equally plausible to assume that individuals who believe that gender equality has not yet been achieved might be motivated toward political engagement in order to promote or enhance their political status. The data shows that as for the Naga women, their perception on gender political inequality is producing what might be called a syndrome of detachment or indifference, resulting in electoral passivity in them.

It is also important to consider the possibility, indeed probability, that the nature of political environment in Nagaland may be an important factor for the disengagement of women in electoral activities. Taking into consideration the nature of the contemporary political culture that exists in present day Nagaland, it is not surprising that women dissociate themselves from politics. Over the years electoral competition in Nagaland has deteriorated in terms of ethics and values. At the time of election, some of the party members and their supporters indulge in all kinds of malpractice and intimidation. Elections are often accompanied by violence, corruption and manipulation. Many women may not be prepared to be involved in a political environment, which supports an aggressive and a combative culture. These phenomena may contribute to a situation where women may reject, dissociate or may be reluctant to become a part of male style politics. For many women, these are probably among the most difficult barriers to overcome. Such a culture may undermine the willingness and enthusiasm of not just women but also men to engage in electoral activities. This kind of political environment may be limiting, constraining or excluding women from participation in politics.

Some of the women described hesitation or discomfort with taking on political and especially public roles. According to them, it feels uncomfortable or inappropriate for them to engage in political activities. This could possibly be due to the reason that women and men are conditioned by society to play different roles. Only certain patterns of behaviour are suitable for women and that politics is not included in these behaviour patterns. This may be another reason why women perceive participating in electoral activities as unsuitable for them.

Compounding these problems is, of course, the resistance women can face once they decide to take on a public role, especially from men. This is corroborated by some women who expressed some kind of experience with resistance from men (husband). There clearly exist biases against women taking part in electoral activities. This could be mainly due to lack of wider public support for women's participation in politics. It is also possible that men do not want to give up their hegemony over political power. The BJP leader and the then Prime Minister, Vajpayee, himself referred to the "general insecurity of menfolk" and their vested interest in "perpetuating male supremacy."[6]

Conclusion

Going beyond the issue of franchise, women's participation in campaigning, attending election meetings, membership in political party and engagement in political discussion has been examined. It appears that Naga women duly go to the polls to register their vote, but their involvement in other electoral activities stops there. Their participation in other modes of electoral activities is just minimal.

It is clear that a number of factors combine to define the functional boundaries of women's mobility, freedom and choice to engage in electoral activities. Their mininal participation in many modes of electoral activities is due to a number of factors: political, socio-cultural and psychological constraints, all of which appear to be too binding for them to overcome. Women's choice to overcome marginalization in politics would probably depend on whether they identify themselves with the perception that society holds about them or to assert an identity in opposition to their wider societal image.

NOTES

1. S. Mitra & James Chiriyankandath (eds) (1992), *Electoral Politics in India: A Changing Landscape.* Segment Book, New Delhi.
2. William R. Schonfeld, "The Meaning of Democratic Participation." *World Politics*, Vol.28, No.1, 1975, pp.134-158.
3. *Statistical Handbook of Nagaland,* Government of Nagaland, 2001.
4. David E. Campbell and Christina Wolbrecht "See Jane Run: Women Politicians as Role Models for Adolescents." *The Journal of Politics*, Vol. 2, May 2006, pp.233-247.
5. Robert Inglehart., et al. (2001) "Gender Equality and Democracy." *Teaching and Research Review*, Issue 5, winter, 2005.
6. *The Hindu*, March 9, 1999.

5

Political Awareness and Its Implications on Participatory Behaviour

Introduction

The present chapter incorporates the knowledge dimension of women voters. Keeping in view the fact that the health of a democracy is enhanced by an informed, engaged and participatory citizenry, the study have examined how well informed the women voters are about politics, what factors influence their level of awareness about politics and whether their level of political awareness influences their participation in electoral activities. Such an examination becomes pertinent taking into consideration their low level of participation in many modes of electoral activities. It is generally assumed that higher the level of political awareness, higher would be the level of participation in electoral activities. As one increase, so does the other.[1] Therefore, it is reasonable to assume that the level of political awareness of women would have some influence on their pattern of participation in electoral activities.

The concept of political awareness is a broad term in political science literature. It has been discussed using different terminology. Some political scientists refer to the term political awareness as "political sophistication," "political information," "political knowledge," "civic competence," and "political expertise". Using different terms, political scientists have offered different definitions of the term. Some political scientists have defined political awareness as a function of three elements:

(1) Level of exposure to political information,

(2) Intellectual ability to retain and organize the encountered information,

(3) Motivation to obtain and comprehend the political information.[2]

It refers to the extent to which an individual pays attention to politics and understands what he or she has encountered.[3] Using the term political expertise, some political scientist hold that the term includes the interlocking set of knowledge, interest and participation.[4]

Further, using the term political knowledge some authors posit that the term political awareness is a vast concept and cover at least three dimensions. Firstly, information can pertain to the individual's level of the political system. Secondly, information can relate to individuals knowledge of everyday politics. Thirdly and partly intertwined with the second dimension, a voter can possess knowledge of the political actors, persons or parties, and their differences ideologically or in relation to politics.[5] It follows that political awareness is generally concerned with how voters with different levels of political awareness make political decisions, how they decide to vote, how they evaluate the issues and how they judge the performance of the government.

From the above definitions of political awareness, it thus appears that having awareness about politics influences how much and how well citizens will participate in the political process. Since people in a democracy are given the opportunity to exercise influence over public policy and those who formulate it, it stands to reason that people who are unfamiliar with the issues and politics will be less inclined to participate. Less informed segment of the public are – in part because of the lack of knowledge–less able to discern their political interests, less likely to participate in politics, and most importantly, less likely to connect their political interests affectively to their political participation.[6]

It follows that if women have low awareness about politics they can participate in the electoral process only up to a certain extent. Against this background, political awareness is taken as the degree to which the women respondents are knowledgeable about politics and related issues.

The analyses in the present chapter centers on the following questions:

- How well informed are the women voters with regard to politics and related issues
- What factors account for differences in political awareness which may be observed
- To what extent women's level of political awareness influences their participation in electoral activities.

Measurement of Women's Level of Political Awareness

The respondents were asked a number of questions pertaining to factual or current events knowledge, i.e., knowledge about political issues or factors that are relevant in a contemporary political context. It is pertinent to mention here that with respect to participatory behaviour, factual or current-events knowledge fulfils at least three purposes:

- It allows citizens to make informed decisions
- It creates a sense of civic duty among citizens

- It increases familiarity with bureaucratic institutions and political processes.[7]

The respondents were asked questions pertaining to names of public figures, political parties, political institutions and public issues pertaining to Nagaland politics. These questions tap into different areas of political awareness of the respondents. Knowledge of this sort demands a certain level of attention and absorption of what is going on in the political world.

A knowledge scale was calculated to place the respondents in one of the three levels of political awareness. This was calculated by adding the correct answers to the political awareness questions for every individual respondent (voters and non-voters). The knowledge scale ranges from high political awareness, medium political awareness, and low political awareness. Based on the respondent's answers, each correct answer is counted as one (1) point. Those respondents who scored between 1-3 points were placed in 'low political awareness' category, those who scored between 4-6 points in 'moderate political awareness' category, and those securing 7-9 points were placed in 'high political awareness' category.

Table 5.1
Political Knowledge Scale

Knowledge Scale	*Percentage*
High	24.67 (75)
Medium	45.72 (139)
Low	29.61 (90)
Total	100 (304)

As noted, the political knowledge scale has been created by summing the number of correct answers based on the different political awareness questions. None of the respondents answered all questions correctly. As per the data highlighted in Table 5.1, the level of political awareness for majority of the women respondents are balanced around the middle of the knowledge score. It means that political awareness for a large number of women is medium at 45.72 per cent. While 29.61 per cent of the women tend toward the low end of the knowledge score, the number of women falling at the highest end of the knowledge scale is relatively few (24.67 %).

The above data indicate that majority of the women respondents are insufficiently informed about politics and related issues. This is despite the fact that level of education of Naga women is relatively high (61.46 %).[8] A high level of education is expected to lead to an increase in political awareness. It is surprising that just few of them should be aware of events in the news and public life especially relating to politics. Therefore an increase in educational attainment over the past decades by women in Nagaland does not correspond to a commensurate gain in political awareness.

Factors leading to Differences in Level of Political Awareness

Having identified that there is an important amount of variance in the level of political awareness among the women respondents, it remains to account for these differences. This aspect is dealt with in this section. This also forms the second part of analyses on measurement of women's political awareness, i.e., what factors accounts for differences in levels of political awareness among women. An attempt is made to identify specific individual and contextual factors or characteristics which may be associated with differential levels of political awareness–low, medium, and high levels of political awareness. A number of demographic variables are taken into consideration in light of prior research. These variables are supplemented by a number of other factors such as political interest, political discussion, and media exposure of the respondents.

Political awareness and age

The first variable that has been included in order to see how much of an effect it might have on the level of political awareness of women respondents is age. It is expected that age will have a positive effect on political awareness. The older respondents presumably will be more knowledgeable politically than the younger respondents, because as people grow older they may have more exposure to politics. Exposure to politics is often considered as an important source of political information.

The result as shown in Table 5.2 however does not support the contention that political awareness increases with a corresponding rise in age. No consistent rise or fall in the level of political awareness is found with an increase in age. A high level of political awareness is most extensive in the age group of 45-59. Next came the women in 18-29 age group. They are followed by those in the age group of 30-44 and 60 and above respectively.

Table 5.2
Political Awareness and Age

Age	*Level of political awareness*			
	Low	*Medium*	*High*	*Total*
18-29	23.33	46.67	30	100
30-44	25	45.83	29.17	100
45-59	16.47	49.41	34.12	100
60 and above	48.48	33.33	18.19	100

A similar result is indicated in the medium political awareness level. Women in the 45-59 age group have the highest score (49.41 %), followed by the younger women (18-29) who scored 46.67 per cent. The 30-44 age group scored 45.83 per cent and the 60 and above scored 33.33 per cent.

If we look at data for low political awareness, majority of women having low awareness (48.48 %) are the oldest respondents in the sample (60 and above). They are followed by those women in 30-44,18-29 and 45-59 age category respectively. Therefore, the study result does not show strong association between women's age and level of political awareness.

Political awareness and educational qualification

Education affects level of political awareness in many ways. For instance, it provides direct exposure to political information by widening the scope of one's acquaintance with political facts. Such exposure to political information is more extensive among the more educated. Further, those who are more educated may learn more about politics and political issues than the less educated individuals. This may be because through education, people get the capacity necessary to understand and process political information. Further, education helps in developing a sense of civic obligation, which creates interest in politics.[9] Thus, education is expected to be strongly and positively related to women's level of political awareness.

As expected, an increase in education does seem to be associated with an increase in political awareness (Table 5.3). The number of years of formal education has been found to be positively related to level of political awareness. In other words, political awareness is directly proportional to the level of educational qualification of the respondents. Each rise in the level of education is accompanied by a corresponding rise in the level of political awareness of the respondents.

In the high political awareness category, women's degree of awareness increases with a rise in level of education. For instance, among women who do not have any education, only 7.69 per cent scored in the high awareness category. Among women in the next higher category of education i.e., non-metric, 17.35 per cent have high awareness about politics. The under-graduates scored 35.14 per cent and finally women with the highest educational qualification i.e., graduate and above, scored the highest level of political awareness (46.38 %).

Table 5.3
Political Awareness and Educational Qualification

Educational qualification	*Level of political awareness*			
	Low	*Medium*	*High*	*Total*
Illiterate	61.54	30.77	7.69	100
Non-metric	39.79	42.86	17.35	100
Under-graduate	16.21	48.65	35.14	100
Graduate and above	2.90	50.72	46.38	100

In the medium awareness category, level of political awareness for women with no education at all is 30.77 per cent, for the non-metric 42.86 per cent, the under-graduates with 48.65 per cent and 50.72 per cent for the graduate and above.

In the low political awareness column, the illiterates are most extensively represented (61.54 %). They are followed by the non-metric (39.79 %), the under-graduate (16.21 %), and lastly by the graduate and above with just 2.90 per cent. The above result have shown that the percentages of low scorers steadily drops as the educational level rises and the percentages of low score is low among those women who have the highest educational qualification. Therefore, the study establishes a strong association between education and levels of political awareness.

Political awareness and occupational status

It is held that those who are gainfully employed tend to have high levels of political interest, and to be more knowledgeable about politics.[10] This could be due to the fact that occupation of a person is clearly related to the degree of his formal education.[11] Higher levels of education may stimulate increased political interest, which helps to acquire more political knowledge.

From Table 5.4 it can be observed that being gainfully employed have a positive impact on political awareness level. High awareness about politics is most extensive among women who are professionals (39.22 %) and are in service (37.18 %). Percentage of women having high political awareness among those respondents who reported that they were unemployed, i.e., non-earners, is 29.56 per cent. As for women who are cultivators, just 11.67 per cent of them have high awareness about politics and related issues.

Table 5.4
Political Awareness and Occupational Status

Occupational status	*Level of political awareness*			
	Low	*Medium*	*High*	*Total*
Service	12.82	50	37.18	100
Professionals	7.84	52.94	39.22	100
Cultivators	51.66	36.67	11.67	100
Non-earners	26.08	44.35	29.57	100

In the next lower category of political awareness (medium), similar result is indicated. The professionals (52.94 %) hold the highest score for medium political awareness followed by those in service (50 %), non-earners (44.35 %) and the cultivators (36.67 %). Women cultivators, who generally have low level of education, dominate the low political awareness level (51.66 %). In this category, the cultivators are followed by the non-earners (26.08 %), women who are in service (12.82 %) and lastly the professionals (7.84 %). Therefore, a positive association between being gainfully employed and political awareness can be observed among the respondents from the four occupational categories.

Political awareness and marital status

The marital status variable has also been included to see if it has an impact on the amount of political information the respondents have. It is expected that marital status of the respondents will have a positive effect on levels of political awareness, with the married women having higher awareness about politics than the unmarried. This suggestion is made because of the potential of political discussion between the husband and the wife. Even if no political discussion takes place, the political views of the spouse, especially the husband, may have an affect on the views of the other spouse, i.e., wife.

Table 5.5
Political Awareness and Marital Status

Marital status	*Level of political awareness*			
	Low	*Medium*	*High*	*Total*
Married	29.35	46.74	23.91	100
Unmarried	17.5	44.17	38.33	100

However, the result shows that marital status have different impact on different levels of political awareness. As illustrated by Table 5.5, being married does not necessarily lead to high awareness about politics. For instance, reading data from the high political awareness column, the unmarried women have more political awareness (38.33 %) than the married respondents (23.91 %). The reason why married women has less knowledge about politics could possible be due to resource constraint. In order to acquire political information one needs some resource especially in terms of time. There is a strong possibility that focus on the home, children and related responsibilities stand in the way of married women, by either reducing the time available for acquiring political information or by simply reducing their interest in politics.

However, married women (46.74 %) are represented more than the unmarried women (44.17 %) in the medium awareness group. In the low political awareness group, the married women comprise of 29.35 per cent, whereas the unmarried women constitute 17.5 per cent.

Therefore, the result reveals mixed results on the relationship between marital status and levels of political awareness.

Political awareness and place of residence

The urban dwellers as compared to the rural dwellers are expected to be more knowledgeable about political issues. Such a suggestion is advanced because urban areas generally have higher levels of literacy and wider mass media coverage. These factors are considered important in increasing citizen's awareness about issues pertaining to politics.

It is clear from Table 5.6 that women residing in urban areas have higher level of political awareness than women who reside in rural areas.

Table 5.6
Political Awareness and Place of Residence

Place of residence	*Level of political awareness*		
	Low	*Medium*	*High*
Urban	8.76	51.82	39.42
Rural	37.72	40.72	21. 56

The result as reflected in the Table 5.6 show that 39.42 per cent with high awareness and 51.82 per cent of medium information come from women from urban areas. The corresponding percentages for women from rural areas are 21.56 per cent (high awareness) and 40.72 per cent (medium awareness). As expected, women having low awareness come from the rural areas (37.72 %). In this category, women from urban areas are represented by just 8.76 per cent.

Therefore, the above analysis reveals that women who live in urban areas do have higher levels of political awareness than their counterparts from rural areas.

Political awareness and political interest

Generally, political interest has been considered as one of the key variables in explaining levels of political awareness. An interest in politics may be very good predictor of who will or will not participate in the electoral process. Those who are interested in politics will try to acquire and retain political information, which will ultimately lead, in turn, to higher levels of political information and participation. An individual's interest in politics is important because it is interest that supplies the motivation for citizens to follow political events and acquire information. On the other hand, an individual who is not interested in politics is less likely than others to be politically informed.

Women's level of interest in politics was assessed by using the standard question on political interest: "How much interest do you generally have in what is going on in politics?" with responses, "a great deal, some, not at all". As indicated by Fig 5.1, a large number of women (48 %) do not have an interest in politics at all. Another 37 per cent of them evinced some interest in politics and just a minority of women (15 %) reported having a great deal of interest in politics.

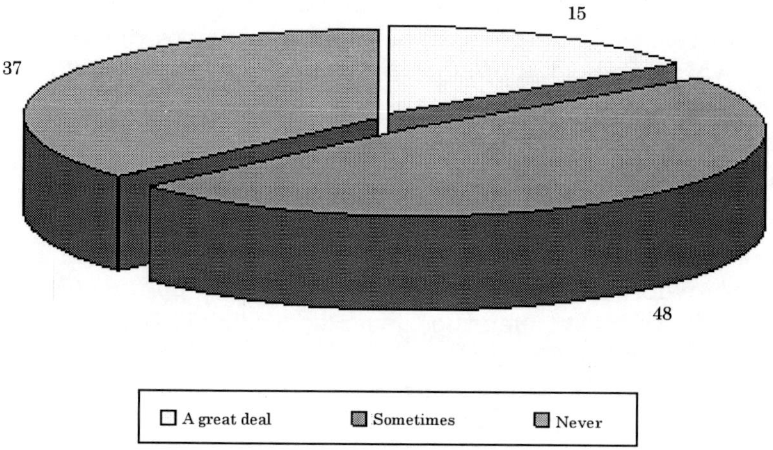

Fig 5.1. Political Interest of the Respondents

The relationship between level of political awareness and political interest is made clearer through further elaboration of Table 5.7. It shows that the effect of political interest is highly significant in determining the level of political awareness of women. The higher the level of women's interest in politics the higher is their level of political awareness. An increased interest in politics appears to stimulate a growth in political awareness. On the contrary, the lower the respondents interest in politics the lower is their level of political awareness.

Table 5.7
Political Awareness and Political Interest

Political interest	*Level of political awareness*			
	Low	*Medium*	*High*	*Total*
Not at all	57.14	27.73	15.13	100
Some	3.68	72.06	24.26	100
A great deal	4.08	16.33	79.59	100

Women who have a great deal of interest in politics also have the highest level of political awareness (79.59 %). This reveals that having an interest in politics definitely leads to an increase in awareness about politics. They were followed by women who have some interest in politics (24.26 %) and those who reported not having any interest in politics have the lowest score in high political awareness category (15.13 %).

Among those who come under the medium political awareness group, an overwhelming number of them are those who indicate having some interest in politics (72.06 %), followed by women those who do not have an interest in politics (27.73 %) and those women having a great deal of interest in politics are least represented in the moderate awareness group (16.33 %).

Looking at data from the low political awareness column, as expected, women who have no interest in politics dominate the group (57.14 %). Women who have some (3.68 %) or a great of interest in politics (4.08 %), are least represented in the low political awareness category. Therefore, the study finds a strong support for the proposition that an interest in politics lead to an increase in political awareness of the respondents.

Political awareness and mass media

The mass media is considered to be an important source of political information. Knowledge of public representatives, political parties, and political issues, has become a cornerstone of democratic societies. People get information on these issues from a variety of sources. The mass media is an obvious source from where people get a lot of information on these issues. It plays a very important role in how much political knowledge an individual gain. Mass media, therefore, can have an impact on political awareness and consequently on women's participation in different forms of electoral activities. This is expected because the mass media, whether television, radio or the newspaper, are considered to be major source of news for many people.

Watching news broadcast on television, listening to radio news or reading a newspaper is likely to increase a person's exposure to political issues and events and thereby increase political knowledge. In fact, the literature review on media effects shows that all forms of media can significantly increase political awareness and thereby engagement in politics. Since people get a great deal of information on politics and related issues through the media, their level of political awareness would be closely related to the degree of media consumption. In other words, increased access and use of media are likely to increase an individual's level of political awareness.

As discussed above, there is no doubt that media plays a very important role in guaranteeing access to political information to the potential voters. Ideally, media is expected to provide at least two sets of information. In the first place, it should try bringing the real issues of the contemporary society to the fore; and secondly, it should also try to provide information about the candidate's ability and credentials vis-à-vis those real issues.[12] This way the media ensures that the voters make responsible and informed choices rather than acting out of ignorance or misinformation.[13]

In order to assess how much of women's level of political awareness can be accounted for by their usage of media, they were asked questions about their frequency of media consumption. Attention to politics in newspaper is captured in a question asking how often the respondent read newspapers, with four responses, "regularly (everyday), quiet often but not regularly (several times a week), seldom (several times a month), and never" While attention paid to political news on television and radio is measured by question about the frequency of viewing and listening to newscasts on television and radio.[14]

Table 5.8
Exposure to Newspaper, Radio and Television

Media outlets	*Frequency of media exposure (%)*				
	Never	*Seldom*	*Sometimes*	*Frequently*	*Total*
Newspaper	11.84	22.04	35.86	30.26	100
Radio	15.13	31.91	27.63	25.33	100
Television	16.78	27.30	33.55	22.37	100

Table 5.8 shows the result regarding the frequency of women's exposure to the three media outlets. It appears that newspaper is the major media source from where majority of the women collect information about politics, followed by the radio and television respectively.

A media exposure index was devised, i.e., high, moderate, low and no media exposure, basing on the responses given by the respondents. This was done to place the respondents in one of the four media exposure index. The respondents in the 'high exposure' category are those who watch/listen to news programmes on television and radio, and read newspaper regularly (daily). Persons in the 'moderate exposure' category are those who are often but not regularly (several times a week) exposed to the three media outlets, those who are seldom (several times a month) exposed to the three media outlets belong to the 'low exposure' category, and those who never watch or listen to television or radio news are placed in the 'no exposure' category.

Table 5.9
Index Score of Mass Media Exposure

Index score	*Percentage*
No exposure	12.5 (38)
Low exposure	31.91 (97)
Moderate exposure	37.83 (115)
High exposure	17.76 (54)

The results illustrated in Table 5.9 reveals that majority of the women are exposed to the different media outlets only moderately (37.83 %). Another 31.91 percent of them come under the low exposure scale, 17.76 per cent under the high exposure scale and 12.5 per cent under the no exposure category. It appears that, women respondents are failing to avail themselves in sufficient numbers of the available media resources to keep themselves informed about political issues. Such a pattern of mass media use by the respondents may be an important factor in explaining why majority of women are just moderately informed about political matters.

Table 5.10 shows how exposure to mass media positively affects women's levels of political awareness. In the high political awareness category, 81.48 per cent of women with high media usage have the highest level of information about politics, followed by women who have moderate exposure to media (37.78 %) and women with low media exposure (12.37 %). Not a single woman having no exposure to any of the media outlets, have high knowledge about political matters.

Table 5.10
Political Awareness and Mass Media Exposure

Media exposure	*Level of political awareness*			
	Low	*Medium*	*High*	*Total*
No exposure	86.84	13.16	00.00	100
Low exposure	31.96	55.67	12.37	100
Moderate exposure	9.56	60.87	37.78	100
High exposure	00.00	18.52	81.48	100

In the medium political awareness group, women with moderate media exposure are the high scorers (60.87 %), followed by women who have low media exposure (55.67 %), those with high media exposure (18.52 %) and no media exposure (13.16 %).

None of the women having high media exposure come under the low political awareness category. This category is dominated by women with no exposure to mass media (86.84 %). Some number of women having low (31.96 %) to medium (9.56 %) media exposure also come in this group.

Therefore, the level of media exposure among women appears to be closely associated with their levels of political awareness. These results may be one of the important factors in explaining why women are only moderately informed about politics.

Political Awareness and Political Discussion

Women's participation in political discussion with others have also been included to find out whether it has any relation with their level of political awareness. This is a very important variable because political discussion may lead to more knowledge. If one engages in political discussion with others, they show an interest in politics and some level of knowledge. They are exposed to other people's views and have the potential of being educated in the process. Therefore, political discussion is expected to have a positive and strong impact on political awareness.

Table 5.11
Political Awareness and Political Discussion

Frequency of political discussion	*Level of political awareness*			
	Low	*Medium*	*High*	*Total*
Frequently	6.75	40.54	52.70	100
Sometimes	22.86	47.14	30	100
Never	62.22	38.89	0	100

The proposition that political discussion enhances political awareness is eminently plausible. As highlighted in Table 5.11, high degree of political awareness is most extensive, as expected, among women who discuss politics frequently (52.70 %). The percentages of such high scorers drop steadily as the frequency of political discussion decreases. Among women who talk about politics sometimes, 30 per cent of them have high political awareness. None of the women who never discuss politics have high level of political awareness.

Medium level of awareness about politics is most widespread among women who discuss about politics with others sometimes (47.14 %). They are followed by women who discuss politics frequently (40.54 %). Those who never discuss politics are represented in this category by 38.89 per cent.

As expected, those who never discuss about politics dominate the sample among low political awareness scorers.

Maximum number of them has low awareness about politics (62.22 %). They are followed by those who discuss politics sometimes (22.86 %) and the least number of women in low political awareness group are those who frequently discuss politics (6.75 %).

Therefore, the above data reveals that frequency of discussing politics with others does lead to a higher level of political awareness.

Political Awareness and Electoral Participation

This section deals with the relationship, if any, between women's level of political awareness and participation in electoral activities. This is illustrated by the result displayed in Table 5.12. The first column consists of various variables representing individual socio-economic factors. Data for electoral participation as illustrated in the Table is the average percentage of women's participation in different modes of electoral activities—voting, campaigning for candidate, attending election meetings, party membership and political discussion. In analyzing the data, 'never' responses to political discussion question was not calculated since this implies non-participation.

The results on the relationship between political awareness and electoral participation become clear in Table 5.12. If we analyse the data according to age groups then we find that women between 46-59 years are the most active participants, although almost half of them fall in the 'moderate' political awareness category. Level of educational attainment shows a positive relationship with political awareness, but a negative relationship with electoral participation. Interestingly, on an average, the non-earners are found to be the most active participants from amongst the four occupational categories. However, women professionals are more aware about politics and related issues. If we study the data by marital status, married women participate at a higher rate and also dominate the score on

Table 5.12

Political Awareness and Electoral Participation

Variables	*Participation in electoral activities (%)*	*Levels of political awareness*		
		L	*M*	*H*
Age				
18-29	32.42	23.33	46.68	30
30-44	43.9	25	45.83	29.17
45-59	48.56	16.47	49.41	34.12
60 above	30.71	48.48	33.33	18.19
Educational qualification				
Illiterate	39.38	61.54	30.77	7.69
Non-matric	40.26	39.79	42.86	17.35
Under-graduate	37.58	16.21	48.65	35.14
Graduate above	34.32	2.90	50.72	46.38
Occupational status				
Service	32.57	12.82	50	37.18
Professionals	29.76	7.84	52.94	39.22
Cultivators	39.38	51.66	36.67	11.67
Non-earners	46.43	26.08	44.35	29.57
Marital status				
Married	56.85	29.35	46.74	23.91
Unmarried	43.20	14.5	44.17	38.33
Place of residence				
Urban	44.71	8.76	51.82	39.42
Rural	55.14	37.72	40.72	21.56
Total	41.14	26.56	44.55	28.89

moderate awareness as compared to unmarried women. But if we take data for high awareness, unmarried women take the lead. A comparative analysis of data by place of residence shows that the average percentage of electoral participation by women from rural area is higher than their counterparts in urban areas. However, the later are more aware about political issues than the former.

While there are limits to this analysis, it is difficult to discount the possibility that political awareness may indeed exert influence on women's participatory behaviour. But as these results suggest, political awareness does not seem to have significant impact in explaining the degree of participation among the women voters of Nagaland. Therefore, it is important to consider the possibility, indeed probability, that women's participation is not so much dependent on political awareness but can be traced both historically and contemporaneously to the kind of political environment and socio-cultural values and practices that are firmly entrenched in the existing systems and structures of society.

Conclusion

In this chapter, level of women's political awareness was assessed by a measure of political knowledge questions. The study found that political awareness for majority of the women is balanced around the middle of the knowledge score. Restated, political awareness for majority of the women is medium.

The study found that the respondents showed differences in their level of political awareness and these differences are produced by different influences. On examination it was found that among all the factors, which account for differences in levels of political awareness, factors such as respondent's level of educational qualification engagement in political discussion, political interest, and patterns of media use have strong impact on the amount of political information women have.

Another finding that emerges is the apparently limited impact of political awareness on electoral participation. This does not mean that political awareness is not important or relevant, but that, political awareness is not a sufficient condition for electoral participation for women voters of Nagaland.

NOTES

1. Delli Carpini, Micheal, X., and Scott Keeter (1996), *What Americans Know About Politics and Why it Matters.* New Haven: Yale University Press, p.186.
2. Robert C Luskin (1990), "Explaining Political Sophistication", *Political Behaviour* 12:335.
3. John R. Zaller (1992), *The Nature and Origins of Mass Opinion.* New York: Cambridge University Press.
4. Susan T Fiske, et al. (1983), "The Novice and the Expert: Knowledge Based Strategies in Political Cognition," *The Journal of Experimental Social Psychology,* 19:381-400.
5. Gronlund, K. and Abo Akademi (2005) 'Political Knowledge and the Internet.' Paper presented at the XIV tri-annual Conference of the Nordic Political Association (NOPSA), Reykjavík 11-13, August, 2005.http://registration.yourhost.is/nopsa2005/papers/
6. Delli Carpini, M.X and Ketter, *op. cit.,* p. 177.
7. Wolfinger, R.E., and Rosenstone, S.J. (1980) *Who Votes?* New Haven, CT: Yale University Press.
8. Statistical Handbook of Nagaland, Government of Nagaland, 2001.
9. "Psychological Involvement in Politics." *Elections Archives and International Politics,*Vol.20,November- December, 1989, p.68.
10. Rosenstone, S.J. "Economic Adversity and Voting Turnout." *American Journal of Political Science,* 26, (1982), p.33.
11. M.L.Goel, *op.cit.,* p.60.
12. Abu Nasar Saied Ahmed et al. (2006) *Election Politics in Assam: Issues, Trends and Peoples Mandate.* Akansha Publishing House, New Delhi, p.261.
13. USAID, "The Role of Media in Democracy: Strategic Approach", Centre for Democracy and Governance, Bureau of Global Programs, Field Support, and Research, Washington, D.C., June, 1999
14. Respondents were asked, "How often do you watch/listen to the television and radio broadcast about Politics/issues/activities of the government?" with responses, "a great deal, sometimes, and never".

6

Summary and Conclusion

Keeping in mind the multidimensional nature of political participation, the study going beyond voting has examined women's participation in different modes of electoral activities. The study also examined women's level of political awareness.

In voting behaviour studies, a number of resources have been considered as important variables in affecting the level of citizen's engagement in the electoral process. Such resources include the various aspects of socio-economic status like age, educational qualification, economic status, marital status, occupational status and place of residence, i.e., urban-rural. Similarly, higher level of cognitive resources, such as political awareness, is also considered an important factor in determining how and to what extend citizens will participate in politics. Further, indicators of political engagement such as media exposure and political interest facilitates higher levels of citizens involvement in political activities. All these aspects have been dealt with in the study. The study has been able to identify the variables that are positively associated with different aspects of voting behaviour of women in Nagaland.

The socio-economic profile of the women voters have been identified as a necessary backdrop of the study. Factors such as age, education, occupation, marital status and place of residence have been used in the study. The income variable was not studied because information provided in the questionnaire regarding income was not sufficient enough for a reasonable analysis and conclusion to be made. Majority of the women respondents belong to the age group of 30-44 years, followed by those in the age group of 18-29, 45-59 and 60 and above (Fig 3.1). A large number of them are married (Fig 3.3). Further, majority of women come under the educational category of under graduates, followed by the non-metric, graduate and above and the illiterates (Fig 3.2). In order to maintain a comparative perspective, urban and rural respondents were represented by 46 per cent and 54 per cent respectively.

Their profile further indicates that, among those who are gainfully employed, majority of them are employed in Government service, a moderate number of them are professionals and some are engaged in agricultural activities. Majority of the women in the sample are non-earners - housewives, students and unemployed (Fig 3.4). As the level of women's work participation has a direct bearing on their overall status in the society, their occupational profile may be indicative of the present low economic status of the Naga women in general.

The hypothesis about socio-economic factors as a variable in voting has been built around the assumption that, socio economic factors effect voting participation of citizens and that, higher the socio-economic status of the voter, higher would be the rate of their participation in voting. However, the study reveals that this assumption holds true for only certain variables.

Taking age as a variable, the study indicates large differences in voting participation by age. In the study, women below 30 years are less likely to vote. They recorded the lowest voting rate. The most politically active age groups for voting are those women in the age group of 45-59 years. They are most active as voters, recording the highest voting turnout. However, voting frequency slightly declines for the 60 and above age group (Table 3.7).

Education is one of the most often cited explanations of electoral participation. Individuals with higher education generally have a higher propensity to vote. This is because education is widely believed to facilitate the acquisition of civic skills and knowledge that lead to participation in politics. The overall level of educational attainment of Naga women has increased in recent decades. This trend should have produced an increase in voting turnout. Yet the study observes precisely the opposite. Contrary to the expected pattern, the positive association between education and voting was not observed among the more educated respondents covered in the study. Women with no education or women with low to moderate education recorded the highest turnout. Women who are more educated appear to be abstaining themselves from voting (Table 3.8). Therefore, education does not influence the turnout rate of women voters.

Further, findings of the study do not show a clear picture of any significant association between women's occupational status and voting. Among all the occupational categories, the non-earners recorded the highest voting turnout. They were followed by women who are in service. Women engaged in agricultural activities also show a higher propensity to vote. Women professionals were found to be the least active as voters (Table 3.9).

Another observation from the study analysis is that, marital status appears to be positively associated with voting, with married women being more active as voters than the unmarried women (Table 3.10).

The study findings also did not confirm the prevailing established observation that urban dwellers are more likely to vote than the rural dwellers. The study reveals that women from the rural areas are more active than women from urban areas as far as voting participation is concerned. The rural turnout clearly exceeds urban turnout (Table 3.11).

Therefore the study finds that, among the socioeconomic variables only age and marital status have strong association with women's propensity to vote. Contrary to earlier studies, women having no education and low to moderate education, the non-earners and women who reside in rural areas tend to vote at high rate.

There is no doubt that Naga women's participation in voting is very high. The voting rate for women in the study is 82 per cent (Fig 3.6). It is clear that the all male lawmakers in Nagaland are voted to power on the strength of women vote. In this context, women need to be made aware that they could use their voting strength as a powerful political resource, by way of voting women to elective office.

Despite the fact that women voters in Nagaland vote in large numbers and they also constitute almost half of the voting constituency, till date not a single woman candidate was ever elected to the State Legislature. This indicates that the Naga electorate in general and the women voters in particular are not voting in favor of the women candidates. This finding is reflective of the fact that women voters do not exercise their franchise independently. Majority of the women voters vote under family influence (Table 3.12). They deem discussion among family members as important factor in determining their vote decision.

The reason why many women do not vote independently is linked to who makes decisions in the household. This explanation highlights the fact that, it is the male members of the household who decide the choice of candidate/party for the family. Most of the women remain excluded from participation in important decisions making in the family (3.13). Such decisions are mostly taken by the husband or the father. Such a gendered power relations at home obviously affect the way women behave in the public space. This connection may be implicit and not clearly connected even in the women's mind. But it appears that the existence of patriarchal power at home level is affecting subconsciously women's sense of freedom to make independent decisions, including independent voting decision.

Women's preconceived notions of gender role stereotypes may also influence their voting choice. Like any other patriarchal society, gender role stereotyping is still prevalent in the Naga society, where women and men are expected by tradition to play different roles. In Naga society, though men and women enjoy equal status, the norms and attitudes regarding a women's role in society is traditional. Leadership role is still conceptualized as a preserve of men and women's role is largely deemed to be in the household. As women are socialized in terms of their gender roles in society, they become more or less conscious of their role in the public political arena. Such a cultural learning, partly explains why women perceive women candidates as less qualified than men to run for public office, leading women voters to vote for the male candidates. Therefore, Naga women's success in election depends not so much on the electorate at large, but on how society as a whole perceives women in public political role.

In the case of the hypothesis that, Naga women's participation is confined more to voting, the result is conclusive. To test the above hypothesis a number of socio-economic and demographic variables that the literature survey has established as important correlates of political participation, such as, age, education, occupation, marital status, and place of residence, have been employed. Despite the fact that Naga women are very active as voters, they are much harder to enlist in other modes of electoral activities (Table 4.6). Voting is no doubt one of the most basic forms of electoral activity in a participatory democracy. However, electoral politics being multidimensional, the scope of electoral activities extends beyond voting. In the study, four types of electoral activities taps into women's participation in other modes of electoral activities. They include campaigning for political party or candidate, attending election meetings, party membership and taking part in political discussion.

Taking age as a variable, the study indicates women in the 45-59 age group as the most active participants in all indices of electoral activities (Table 4.1), including voting. The participation rate of women in the 18-29 age category is just moderate. The apathy among younger women is a cause of concern, keeping in mind the fact that participatory norm among the women electorate, as a whole is quiet low, except for voting. The present trend of low electoral participation among the young women would continue into the future, as the younger women would replace the older generation. Therefore it is important that young women are encouraged to participate more effectively in the electoral process. The older women (60 and above) as compared to the young, are found to be more active in discussing politics and attending meeting. But their participation declines when it comes to the more active forms of electoral activities. This is explained by the fact that as individuals grow older opportunities for being active in political activities are reduced.

Contrary to earlier studies, as educational level of women goes up, participation rate in campaigning, election meetings and party membership comes down. In these modes of electoral activities, women with no education and low to moderate level of education are found to be the most active participants, while the low participants are those women with the highest level of education. However, when it comes to political discussion, the picture is changed. For instance, frequency of political discussion increases with an increase in the level of education (Table 4.2). To engage in political discussion one needs to have some amount of information about politics and related issues. Since the educated women presumably possess more information about politics, they are expected to take part in political discussion more frequently than the less educated. But it is clear that they do not extend this kind of participatory norm to the more public forms of electoral activities, such as campaigning for a candidate/party, attending election meetings and to a lesser extent party membership. Therefore the highly educated are found to be behaviorally passive but politically informed.

Women from lower occupational group (non-earners, students, housewives and unemployed) are more active in campaigning, attending election meetings and party membership (Table 4.3). The participation of women from higher occupational status, like the professionals and those in government service, tend to confine more to the less public political activity like political discussion. The study also indicates that marital status determines women's involvement in electoral activities, with the unmarried women being less active in all indicators of electoral activities as compared to the married women (Table 4.4).

The urban-rural differences on participation in various forms of electoral activities show mixed results. Women residing in urban areas are more exposed to various channels of urbanization like the mass media and better educational facilities, factors which are believed to facilitate participation in political activities. Surprisingly, urbanization does not seem to have any impact on the urban dwellers, by way of enhancing their participation level in campaigning, attending election meetings and party membership. In these activities, women from the rural areas seem to outpace women from urban areas. However, compared to women from rural areas, the urban residents engage more in political discussion (Table

4.5). Therefore, the electoral activity of the urban women is confined more to political discussion.

Therefore, the key finding is simply disengagement of women in different modes of electoral activities, except voting. Thus, women in Nagaland have been able to strengthen their political visibility only as voters. This validates the hypothesis that participation of Naga women is confined more to voting. The more public the electoral activity, the lesser the rate of women's participation. Though voting is considered as a public political act, women's participation in voting is quiet high. It is possible that there exists different social prescription for women's participation in different electoral activities. Therefore, it is safe to assume that, positive encouragement from the society would facilitate women's participation in all forms of political public activity.

Majority of women opines that, in order to enhance the number of women in politics, the initiative should come from the society. This observation made by the respondent's show how much impact social structures have on women's involvement in politics. Therefore, the societal prescription of what constitute the private and public space may be at the heart of some of the limitations and difficulties faced by women in taking part in electoral process.

Besides, there are some more reasons why women are not able to sustain their participation in electoral activities beyond voting. Women themselves evince less interest in politics (Fig 5.1). Having interest in politics is considered an important factor in motivating people to participate in political activities. However, the reality that is often overlooked is that, despite major changes in gender roles in recent decades in Nagaland, women are still largely expected to look after the household responsibilities. Indeed, much of the time that some may have wished to devote to political activities is taken up by their maternal and domestic responsibilities. Time is one of the resources required to involve in political activities. The possibility remains that focus on the home and family stand in the way of women's engagement in electoral activities, either by reducing the time available for such activities or reducing their interest in politics.

The negative image associated with contemporary politics in Nagaland deters many women from participating in the electoral process. This is mainly because electoral competition in Nagaland has deteriorated in terms of values and ethics. Women who take part in politics are generally subjected to a lot of public scrutiny as regard their moral character.

In Nagaland, gender stereotyping of roles becomes quiet prominent when the subject is politics. Electoral activities, such as campaign activities which take place in a public arena are usually assigned for male members of the society. Women on the other hand are assigned specific roles centered around children, family and private life. Therefore, the belief that politics is an inherently men's domain, has impacted negatively on women's involvement in political process, a fact reflected by the low participation by women in the electoral activities. Further, unlike their male counterparts, women do not receive encouragement from the society at large for involvement in politics. Women themselves are conscious of such limitations.

Though Naga women enjoy an equal status with men in the society, they have not yet achieved a comparable status with men in politics. In terms of sheer numbers and positions of importance, men dominate the power structures and institutions in Nagaland. The state legislature, the village councils and the political parties are all democratic bodies that are supposed to be a means for all citizens to be equally represented or involved in democratic processes. It appears that in Nagaland, men's domination in the public sphere is being reproduced within participatory and democratic bodies as well. Till date there has been no women representative in the state legislature. At the grassroots level, the village council is the highest decision making body. Women, by tradition are not allowed to take part in the decision making process of the village councils. Women are therefore denied to play a political role in these bodies.

The representation of women in qualitative terms, that is, in party leadership and influence over party decision is also absent. Among the women respondents who are members of political party, very few of them have higher status in the party hierarchy, as members of the party executive or as office bearers. Most of the political parties mobilize women voters just for their vote. Some of the women party activists who had been interviewed expressed dissatisfaction with the gendered division of labour within the party structure. They opined that, besides casting their vote for the party, their work is confined to preparing meals, providing help in organizing meetings, doing voluntary work in party office and distributing material goods to the prospective voters during election campaign. This indicates that commitment of political parties to the advancement of women is very much of a token nature. They mobilize women just for securing their votes. How political parties in Nagaland are reaching out to women is beyond the scope of the present work, but it is an area worth monitoring for future research in the interest of equalizing the political status of women with that of men, at least in terms of representation.

Keeping in view the fact that the health of a democracy is enhanced by an informed, engaged and participatory citizenry, the study have examined how well informed the women voters are about politics, what factors influence their level of awareness about politics and whether their level of political awareness influences their participation in electoral activities. Political awareness for the study is taken as the degree to which women are knowledgeable about politics and related issues. Awareness about political issues creates an interest in politics. In turn, an interest in politics induces political involvement.

The level of political awareness of the women voters was measured by a political knowledge scale that was constructed using the conventional approach, i.e., by awarding respondents one point for each correct answer. The incorrect and don't know response's were coded as zero.

It was hypothesized that political awareness of Naga women voters is high. This hypothesis was formulated taking into consideration the high level of literacy among women in Nagaland (61.92 %, 2001 Census). Several studies have indicated that education is a strong predictor of political knowledge. The higher the level of education, the higher would be the level of political knowledge. However, the hypothesis that Naga women's political awareness is high has not been sustained in the study. Majority of the women voters, as the study reveals, have moderate level of awareness about politics and related issues. The number of women who have high level of political awareness is few (Table 5.1). It appears that majority of the women are moderately informed about issues in the news and public life relating to politics. The increase in educational attainment over the past decades by women in Nagaland does not correspond to a commensurate gain in political awareness.

According to the study, several factors play a critical role in influencing the level of political awareness of the women voters. Women level of education, occupation, place of residence, discussing politics with others, having an interest in politics and mass media sources of information play a crucial role in enhancing the level of political awareness. However, the study documents a limited influence of political awareness on electoral participation.

Engaging in political discussion with others is one way of gaining political information. Besides, political discussion is also known to encourage positive democratic attitudes and participatory skills. The present study indicates a positive association between political awareness and frequency of political discussion. Despite minimal number of women who discuss politics frequently, there is still abundant evidence which indicate that engaging in political discussion lead to an increase in political awareness. Women who participate in political discussion with others have higher levels of political awareness than women who participate in political discussion with others less frequently (Table 5.11). Such a finding affirms the positive role political discussion play in promoting awareness about politics.

A voter's information about political issues, events, parties or candidates is affected by an interest in politics. It is only when someone has an interest in politics that they will pay attention to political information and presumably, will be more knowledgeable about politics. The level of political awareness of women depends upon their level of interest in politics. Though the number of women who reported having a great deal of interest in politics is marginal, they have the highest level of awareness about politics. Those women who have no interest in politics at all are also the ones having the lowest level of political information (Table 5.7). If there is no interest in politics then there will be no motivation to become more informed.

Mass media is regarded as a very important factor in enhancing political awareness of the people. It can have an impact on voting and other forms of electoral activities. In the recent past, in Nagaland, there has been a major growth in the range of media options available to the people. Voters get a great deal of information about political issues, parties and candidates from various media outlets, like the newspaper, radio and television. Attention to political information in the media increase political knowledge. Majority of women have moderate exposure to the various media outlets (Table 5.8). The pattern of media consumption of women may explain why women are only moderately informed about politics. Restated, moderate exposure to mass media produces moderate awareness of politics.

The study finds that moderate level of political awareness among women is generally attributed to their lack of interest in politics, less interest to engage in political discussion and moderate exposure to news broadcast on television, radio and newspaper.

Reference may be made once again to the major findings of the present study. Both from the survey data and official statistics, analysis show that women's participation in voting is high. Some of the findings regarding the association between different aspects of socio economic status and women's participation in the electoral process are contrary to some common assumption. Education, occupational status and place of residence are not found to have much impact on voting and other electoral activities. This reveals that other factors in addition to some socio-economic attributes of the women electorate, affect the nature and extent of women's participation in electoral activities.

The analysis also reveals that women have moderate level of political awareness. This is attributed to their lack of interest in politics, less exposure to news in the media and little interest in discussing politics with others. This finding may pose some important challenges for women. If they want a more responsive type of politics, they should be willing to play their part as political participants.

As the study indicates a low participatory norm among women, some suggestions arise from the survey findings and if acted upon, it could go a considerable way towards enhancing participatory norms among women.

As per the responses of the respondents, cultural barriers are seen as major impediments towards their participation in politics. This finding show how much of an impact society has on women's participation in politics. Towards this end, public awareness that address gender equality in politics and public life must be taken up. The media can be one of the key players in the task of educating the public and spreading information on gender equality. Besides, the media should also highlight issues relating to women and more importantly make visible the aspiring women politicians. This can have a positive impact on society in general and the women in particular by generating significant interest in political activity among women.

The role of NGO's in motivating women to participate in politics becomes critical from the point of two issues. Firstly, membership in NGO's is found to impact positively on women's involvement in the political process and secondly for many women NGO's may be the only outlet to participate in public space. The women NGO's should organize advocacy campaigns to promote women's participation in politics. The potential women candidates aspiring for political office should be given support base by them. Moreover, they must work towards building political awareness among women. Towards this end, networking amongst the various women NGO's must be developed, so that they can share information and experiences that will enhance the participation of women in politics.

Study shows that visible women politicians have a role model effect on a wide range of political activities among women. In this connection, there can hardly be a stronger argument for gender parity in representation, in a state where women, who constitute half of the population, have been consistently sidelined in public life to the extent that they have never held positions in elective office. Since the number of women candidates largely determine the number of women elected, it is clear that political parties must rise to the challenge by recruiting and supporting female candidates. They should support women within its leadership structures, initiate steps to increase the presence of women in different spheres of political decision-making and undertake programmes of gender equality through its political activities.

Since gender awareness take roots in early childhood, school curricula can play a positive role in bringing about a change towards a gender-equal culture. Textbooks have a major socialization role in the development of children. In this connection, a review of school textbooks at the primary and secondary level, by way of changing stereotypical image of gender roles in the school textbooks and accompanying illustrations, may be taken up wherever possible. This may have positive results by way of inculcating equal values to both boys and girls right from childhood.

Since lack of an adequate, well managed data hampers efforts to accurately identify what aspects of gender issues need to be studied, there is a need to compile gender-disaggregated data and generate databases through micro studies and documentation on the political, social and economic aspects relating to both the genders. Such data would be useful for monitoring as well as bringing about appropriate policy decision, and to provide credible information to both the policy makers and the media.

On the part of women, in order to overcome their marginality in politics, they have to overcome the psychology of subordination in politics. This may depend on whether they choose to identify with the perception that society holds about them or assert an identity in opposition to the wider societal image. It is also imperative that women develop a favourable attitude towards politics, be assertative in their demands and also develop an interest in politics.

There also should be a change in the mind set of the people at large towards women's participation in politics. If such a positive change of attitude towards women's involvement is brought about, it can socialize women into democratic participatory citizens.

It is hoped that the results of the study and suggestions thereof will lead to a consensual agreement on how to empower women politically and see to their emergence as active political participants and leaders in Nagaland.

Bibliography

Primary Sources

Census of India, Nagaland, Directorate of Census Operation, Kohima.

Government of India. Towards Equality, Report of the Committee on the Status of Women in India, Department of Social Welfare, December 1974.

Report on the First General Election to the Nagaland Legislative Assembly, 1964, Government of Nagaland.

Report on the Second General Election to the Nagaland Legislative Assembly, 1969, Government of Nagaland.

Report on the Third General Election to the Nagaland Legislative Assembly, 1974, Government of Nagaland.

Report on the Fourth General Election to the Nagaland Legislative Assembly, 1977, Government of Nagaland.

Report on the Fifth General Election to the Nagaland Legislative Assembly, 1982, Government of Nagaland.

Report on the Sixth General Election to the Nagaland Legislative Assembly, 1987, Government of Nagaland.

Report on the Seventh General Election to the Nagaland Legislative Assembly, 1988-89, Government of Nagaland.

Report on the Eighth General Election to the Nagaland Legislative Assembly, 1993, Government of Nagaland.

Report on the Ninth General Election to the Nagaland Legislative Assembly, 1998, Government of Nagaland.

Report on the Tenth General Election to the Nagaland Legislative Assembly, 2003, Government of Nagaland.

Report on the Eleventh General Election to the Nagaland Legislative Assembly, 2008, Government of Nagaland.

Statistical Hand Book of Nagaland 2001, Government of Nagaland.

Statistical Report on General Elections, 1964-2008, to the Legislative Assembly of Nagaland, Election Commission of India, New Delhi.

Books

Abramson, P.R. (1983), *Political Attitudes in America: Formation and Change*. H.Freeman and Company, San Francisco.

Abu Nasar Saied Ahmed, *et al.* (2006), *Election Politics in Assam: Issues, Trends and Peoples Mandate*. Akansha Publishing House, New Delhi.

Agnew, V. (1979), *Elite Women in Indian Politics*. Vikas Publishing House, Pvt. Ltd.

Ahmed, I. (1975), "Women in Politics, in Jain", D.(ed), *Indian Women,* Publications Division, Ministry of Information and Broadcasting, Government of India, New Delhi.

Ali, R. (1996), *Representative Democracy and Concept of Free and Fair Elections*. Deep & Deep Publications, New Delhi.

Almond, G., and S.Verba. (1963), *The Civic Culture: Political Attitudes and Democracy in Five Nations*. Princeton University Press, New Jersey.

Berelson, B, Paul F.L., and N.W.Mcphee. (1954), *Voting*. The University of Chicago Press, Chicago.

Borgatta,E.F & M.C.Borgatta (eds) *Encyclopedia of Sociology*, Vol 4, p.2230. MacMillan Publishing Company, New York, 1992.

Burns,N.,K.S Lehman, and S.Verba (2001), *The Private Roots of Public Action*. Cambridge, MA: Harvard University Press.

Butler, D., & Hustin Ranney (ed) (1992), *Electioneering: A Comparative Study of Continuity and Change*. Clarendon Press, Oxford.

Campell, A., Converse, P.E., Miller, W.E., and Stokes,D.E. (1960), *The American Voter*. Wiley, New York.

Carpini, D.M.X., and K. Scott (1996), *What Americans Know About Politics and Why it Matters*. Yale University Press, New Haven.

Chandra, P. (2005), *Political Dynamics of Women*. Akansha Publishing House, New Delhi.

Chasie, C. (1999), *The Naga Embroglio*. Standard Printers and Publishers, Kohima.

Chatterjee, P. (ed.) (1997), *State and Politics in India*. Oxford University Press, New Delhi.

Chaube, S.K. (1985), *Electoral Politics in Nagaland*. Sangam Books Limited, New Delhi.

Chaudhuri, S.N. (1995), *Women and Politics, West Bengal: A Case Study*. Minerva Associates Publications Pvt Ltd.

Clark, M. (1896), *Ao Naga Women*. Boston.

Conway, M.M. (1991), *Political Participation in the United States*. Washington: A Division of Congressional Quarterly Inc.

Dalton, R,J. (1996), *Citizens and Politics: Public Opinion and Political Parties in Advanced Western Democracies*. Chatham, NJ,Chatham House.

Das,P.S. (1999), *New Perspectives on South Asian Women*. Book Enclave, Jaipur.

Das, B., & L.N. Dash (1995), *The Feminine Gender*. Manak Publications Pvt. Ltd, New Delhi.

Dasgupta, U. (1994-95), *Pattern of Political Awareness among Women: A Case Study of Greater Guwahati Area*. Institute of Social Change and Development, Guwahati.

Deka, K.M., *et al.* (1987), *A Study of the Sixth General Election to the Assam Legislative Assembly*. 1st Edition, ICSSR Project Report.Bani Prakesh, Guwahati.

Desai, N., & Usha Thakkar. (2001), *Women in Indian Society*. National Book Trust, India, New Delhi.

Downs, F.S. (1996), *The Christian Impact on the Status of Women in North East India*. Published by North-Eastern Hill University Publications, Shillong.

Edward S.Greenberg & Benjamin I. Page. (2002), *The Struggle for Democracy*, Fifth Edition. Addison-Wesley Educational Publishers Inc.

Eldersveld, S.J., & Bashiruddin Ahmed (1978), *Citizens and Politics—Mass Political Behavior in India*. Chicago: University of Chicago.

Encyclopedia Britannica (1965), Vol.23, Inc.William Benton, Publishers, Chicago.

Enclow, J., and M. Hinick. (1984), *The Spatial Theory of Voting*. Cambridge University Press, Cambridge.

Eulau,H.,Roger Gibbins and Paul David Webb. "Election" in *Encyclopedia Britannica* 2004.http://www.britannica.com/eb/article?tocld=36693

Eulau, H., Eldersveld,S.J., and J.Morris. (eds) (1972), *Political Behaviour*. Amerind Publishing Company, New Delhi.

Fatima, E.S. (1999), *Political Women: Country Experiences in Identity and Gender Debate*. Kanishka Publishers, New Delhi.

Forbes, G. (1998), *Women in Modern India*. Cambridge University Press, Cambridge.

Ganguly, B. & M.Ganguly (1975), *Voting Behaviour in a Developing Society*. Sterling Publishers, New Delhi.

Ganguly, B & M. Ganguly (1980), *Role of Women in the Political Process:West Bengal Assembly Election 1977*, (Unpublished) ICSSR Report.

Goel, M.L. (1974), *Political Participation in a Developing Nation: India*. Asia Publishing House, New Delhi.

Goel, M.L. (1980), Conventional Political Participation. In D.H. Smith et al. (eds) *Participation in Social and Political Activities,* Jossey-Bass Publishers, San Francisco.

Gowalini, R.R. (1993), *General Elections to the Assam Legislative Assembly (1978-1985): A Study in Electoral Politics and Voting Behaviour*. Unpublished Ph.D.Thesis, Department of Political Science, Gauhati University, Guwahati.

Green,Donald P., Bradley Palmquist and Eric Schickler. (2000), *Partisan Hearts and Minds: Political Parties and the Social Identity of Voters*. New Haven: Yale University Press.

Greenberg, E.S., and B.I.Page (2000), *The Struggle for Democracy*. Fifth Edition, Addison-Wesley Educational Publishers Inc.

Grover, V. (ed) (1997), *Electoral System, Behaviour and Elections*. Deep & Deep Publications, New Delhi.

Guha, S. (1996), *Political Participation of Women in a Changing Society*. Inter-India Publications.

Gupta, R.L. (1972) ,*Politics of Commitment: A Study Based on Fifth General Elections in India*. Trimurti Publications, New Delhi.

Gupta, R.L. (1985), *Electoral Politics in India*. Discovery Publishing House, New Delhi.

H. Meclosky. (1968), "Political Participation". In David E.Sills (ed), *International Encyclopaedia of the Social Sciences*, Vol.12, MacMillan Company and Free Press, USA.

Herbert, E. and R.Garnett (1977), "Electoral Process"in *Encyclopaedia Britannica* (Macro), The University of Chicago Press, USA, Vol.6.

ICSSR, New Delhi, *Studies of the Fourth General Elections*. Popular Press, Bombay, 1956.

Inglehart, R., and P. Norris (2003), *Rising Tide: Gender Equality and Cultural Change Around the World*. Cambridge University Press, New York.

Jain, D. (ed) (1975), "Indian Women", Publications Division, Ministry of Information and Broadcasting, Government of India, New Delhi.

Jamir, N.Talitemjen., and A. Lanunungsang. (2005), *Naga Society and Culture: A Case Study of the Ao Naga Society and Culture*. Published by Nagaland University Tribal Research Centre, Department of Sociology, Hqrs. Lumami.

Jaquette, J. (1974), *Women in Politics*. John Wiley and Sons.

Jena, B.B., & J.K. Baral. (ed) (1989), *Election Politics and Voting Behaviour in India: A Case Study of Orissa*. Delhi: Discovery Publishing House.

Jocelyn A.J. Evans. (2003), *Voters and Voting: An Introduction*. Sage Publications, New Delhi.

Joseph, P.H. (1962), "Elections", *Encyclopaedia of Social Sciences*, Vol.V-VI, Macmillan, New York.

Kashyup, S.C. (ed) (1971), *Elections and Electoral Reforms in India*. New Delhi.

Kaushik, S. (ed) (1993), *Women's Participation in Politics*. Vikas Publications, New Delhi.

Kini, N.G.S. (1997), *Modernization in India: Women Voting Behaviour as index in Electoral System and Elections*. In Virender Grover (ed), Deep and Deep Publications, New Delhi.

Kini, N.G.S., & T.S.Shastri. *Women Voting Behaviour*. (Mimeographed: Nagpur University, 1969)

Kini, N.G.S. (1974), *The City Voters in India—A Study of 1967 General Elections in Nagpur*. Abhinav Publications, New Delhi.

Kogehar, S.V., and R.L.Park (eds) (1956), *Report on the Indian General Elections 1951-55*. Popular Press, Bombay.

Koshy, C.O. (1986), *Electoral Behaviour in the 1982 Assembly Election in Nagaland: A Case Study of Dimapur Constituency*. Unpublished M.Phil.Dissertation, Department of Political Science, N.E.H.U. Shillong.

Kothari, R. (ed) (1970), *Caste in Indian Politics*. Orient Longman Ltd, New Delhi.

Krishnaraj, M., & N. Desai. (1986), *Women and Society in India*. Ajanta Publications, Delhi.

Lawrence, C.N. (2003), *The Role of Political Sophistication in the Decision-Making Process of Voters*. Unpublished Ph.D.Dissertation, University of Mississippi.www. cnlawrence.com/papers/dissertation.pdf.

Lawrence, D.G. (1981), "Towards an Attitudinal Theory of Political Participation." *Polity*, Vol. 14, No.2, Deep Publications, New Delhi.

Lipset, S.M. (1960), *Political Man: The Social Bases of Politics*. John Hopkins University Press, Maryland.

Lodha, N. (2003), *Status of Tribal Women: Work Participation and Decision Making Role in Tribal Society*. Mangal Deep, New Delhi.

Manza, J., and C.Brooks. (1998), *Social Cleavages and Political Change: Voter Alignments and the US Party Coalitions*. Oxford University Press, New York.

Mark E Warren. (1999), 'Democratic Theory and Trust.' In Mark E.Warren (ed) *Democracy and Trust*. Cambridge: Cambridge University Press.

Marshall Gordon. (ed) (1998), *A Dictionary of Sociology*. Oxford Paperback Reference.

Matland, R.E. (1998), "Enhancing Women's Political Participation: Legislative Recruitment and Electoral Systems", in International IDEA, *Women in Parliament: Beyond Numbers,* IDEA: Stockholm.

Mc Closky, "Political Participation." in *Encyclopaedia of Social Sciences*. New York: Macmillan, 1968, Vol.12.

Mehta, A. (2004), *Progressive Women and Political Identity*. Kanishka, New Delhi.

Milbrath, L.W. (1965), *Political Participation*, Rand McNally, Chicago.

Milbrath, L.W. (1969), 'Political Participation and Citizen', in C.J.Larson and P.C.Wasburn, (eds), *Power, Politics and Ideology,* David McKay Co, New York.

Milbrath, L.W., and M.L.Goel. (2nd edition) (1977), *Political Participation: Why and How Do People Get Involved in Politics?* Rand McNally, New York.

Mitra, S. & James Chiriyankandath. (eds) (1992), *Electoral Politics in India: A Changing Landscape.* Segment Book, New Delhi.

Mukhi. H.R. (1997), *Political Sociology*, SBD Publishers Distributors, Delhi.

Nelson, B.R. & Najma Chowdhury. (eds) (1997), *Women and Politics Worldwide.* Oxford University Press, Delhi.

Neuman, W.R. (1986), *The Paradox of Mass Politics: Knowledge and Opinion in the American Electorate.* Cambridge, MA: Harvard University Press.

Niemi, R., and Jane Junn (1998), *Civic Education: What Makes Students Learn.* New Haven: Yale University Press.

Nohlen, D. (1996), *Elections and Electoral Systems.* Macmillan India Limited, New Delhi.

Norris, P. (2002), *Democratic Phoenix: Reinventing Political Activism.* Cambridge University Press, New York.

P. Snehalata. (2002), *Political Empowerment of Women.* Taj Publishing, Delhi.

P. Snehalata. (1990), *Determinants of Political Participation: Women and Public Activity.* Ajanta Publications, Delhi.

P. Adam. 'Minimalist Conception of Democracy: A Defense in Democracy's Value.' In Ian Shapiro & Casiano Hacker-Cordon (eds) 1999, *Democracy's Value.* Cambridge University Press.

P. Sushila (1994), *Women Political Elite: Search for Identity.* Printwell, Jaipur.

Pandhy, K.S., & P.P.,Tripathy (1994), *Voting Behaviour of Tribals in India.* Kanishka Publishers, Distributors, Delhi.

Parry, G., and George Moyser. (1994), *More Participation, More Democracy?* In Beetham, David (ed), *'Defining and Measuring Democracy,'* Sage Publications, London,Thousand Oaks, New Delhi.

Peter, F.Nardulli. (2005), *Popular Efficacy in the Democratic Era: Reexamination of Electoral Accountability in the United States.*1828-2000. Princeton University Press.

Phillips, A. (2002), "The Representation of Women" in *The Polity Reader in Gender Studies,* Polity Press.

Phillips, A. (1995), *The Politics of Presence.* Claredon Press, Oxford.

Phukon, G., & Adil-Ul-Yasin. (eds) (1996,) *Working of Parliamentary Democracy and Electoral Politics in Northeast India.* South Asian Publishers, New Delhi.

Powell Jr.G.Bingham. (2000), *Elections as Instruments of Democracy.* Yale University Press, New Haven.

Pruthi, R., & Bela Rani Sharma. (eds) (1995), *Trends in Women Studies.* Anmol Publications Pvt Ltd, New Delhi.

Przeworski, A. (1999), 'A Defense in Democracy Value.' In Ian Shapiro and Casiano Hacker-Cordon (eds) *Democracy's Value* Cambridge University Press, Cambridge.

Putnam, R.D. (1993), *Making Democracy Work: Civic Traditions in Modern Italy.* Princeton University Press.

Putnam, R.D. (2000), *Bowling Alone: The Collapse and Revival of American Community.* Simon and Schuster, New York.

Quraishi, Z.M. (1979), *Elections and State Politics in India: A Case Study of Kashmir.* Sundeep Prakashan, Delhi.

R. Steven J., & John Mark Hansen. (1993), *Mobilization, Participation, and Democracy in America.* New York: Macmillan Publishing.

Ramchander, M., & K. Lakshmi. (1993), *Women and Politics: A Study in Political Participation.* Booklinks Corporation, Hyderabad, Rawat Publications, Jaipur.

Rose, R., & Mc Allister, I. (1990), *Loyalties of Voters.* Sage Publications, New Delhi.

Rose, R. (ed) (2000), *International Encyclopaedia of Elections.* MacMillan.

Roy, K. (1999), *Women in Indian Politics.* Rajat Publications, Delhi.

Sachchidananda (1976), *The Tribal Voter in Bihar.* National Publishing House, New Delhi.

Sanyu, V. (1996), *A History of Nagas and Nagaland: Dynamics of Oral Traditions in Village Formation.* Commonwealth Publishers, New Delhi.

Seymour Martin Lipset (ed) (1995), *Encyclopedia of Democracy,* Vol. IV. Routledge University Press, Cambridge.

Shapiro, L., & Casiano Hacker- Cordon. (ed) (1999), *Democracy's Value.* Cambridge University Press, Cambridge *Democracy's Value* e.

Shapiro, L., & Casiano Hacker- Cordon. (1999), *Promises and Disappointments: Reconsidering Democracy's Value* in Ian Shapiro and Casiano Hacker- Cordon (eds) "Democracy's Value" Cambridge University Press.

Sheel,C.N. (1989), *Spatial Fragmentation of Political Behaviour in India: A Geographical Perspective on Parliamentary Elections.* Concept Publishing House, New Delhi.

Shukla, D.M. (1979), "Politicisation of Women in Gujarat", in Vina Mazumdar (ed), *Symbols of Power: Studies on the Political Status of Women in India,* Allied Publishers Pvt Ltd, Bombay.

Sirsikar, V.M. (1973), *Sovereigns without Crowns.* Popular Prakashan, Bombay.

Sniderman, P.M., Prody, R.A., & P.E. Tetlock. (1991), *Reasoning and Choice: Explorations in Political Psychology.* Cambridge University Press, Cambridge.

The Mahbub ul Haq Human Development Centre. 'Human Development in South Asia 2000. *The Gender Question.'* Oxford University Press, Oxford.

Topf, R. (1995), 'Electoral Participation.' In Citizens and the States, eds. Hans-Dieter Klingemann and Deiter Fuchs, Oxford University Press, Oxford.

Tripathy, S. (2000), *Political Participation of Women Workers in India: A Study of Orissa.* Vikas Publishing House Pvt. Ltd, New Delhi.

Varma, S.(1997), *Women's Struggle for Political Space.* Rawat Publications, New Delhi.

Varma, S.P., *et al.* (1973), *Voting Behaviour in a Changing Society: A Case Study of the Fourth General Election in Rajasthan*. National Publishing House, Delhi.

Vats, P. (2004), *Political Participation and Attitudinal Transformation of Rural Women*. Abhijeet, Delhi.

Verba, S.,& Norman H. Nie. (1972), *Participation in America: Political Democracy and Political Equality*. Harper and Row Publishers, New York.

Verba, S., Kay Lehman Schlozman., and H.E. Brady. (1995), *Voice and Equality: Civic Voluntarism in American Politics*, Harvard University Press, Cambridge.

Verba, S.,Norman Nie and Jae-on Kim. (1971), *The Modes of Democratic Participation*.Sage.

Verba, S.,,Ahmad, B.,& Bhatt, A. (1971), *Caste, Race and Politics*. Beverly Hills, Sage.

Verma, R.P. (ed) (2000), *Peoples Participation in Indian Politics*. Rajat Publications, New Delhi.

Verma, S.P., & C.P. Bhambri (ed) (1967), *Election and Political Consciousness in India*. Meenakshi Prakashan, Meerut.

Voting Behaviour in *Encyclopedia of Sociology*. (1992), Vol.4, MacMillan Publishing Company, New York.

Wallace, P.,& Roy, R. (ed) (2003), *India's 1999 Elections and 20th Century Politics*. Sage Publications, New Delhi.

Warren, M.E. (1999), *Democratic Theory and Trust*. Cambridge University Press, Cambridge.

Wolfinger, R.E., & S.J.Rosenstone. (1980,) *Who Votes?* Yale University Press, New Haven.

Woshingsky, O.H. (1995), *Culture and Politics: An Introduction to Mass and Elite Political Behaviour*. Englewood Cliffs: Prentice Hall.

Zaller, John R. (1992), *The Nature and Origins of Mass Opinion*. Cambridge University Press, New York.

Articles

Achen, C.H. (1992) "Social Psychology, Democratic Variables and Linear Regression: Breaking the Iron Triangle in Voting Research." *Political Behavior* 14 (3), 195-221.

Ahmes. Z. (2006), 'Bridging the Gap between Gender Socialization and Gendered Political Behaviour: Political Socialization in a Cultural Context.' Prepared for the 2006 Meeting of the American Political Science Association, pp.1-21.

Anderson, R., & A.H and A.Heath. (2000) "Social Cleavages, Attitudes and Voting Patterns: A Comparison of Canada and Great Britain". CREST Working Paper, Number 81, September 2000.http://www.crest.ox.ac.uk.

Aria G. Bernstein. "Gendered characteristics of political engagement in college students" *Sex Roles: A Journal of Research*, March 2005.

B. Kruti. "Impact of Identity Politics on Differential Voter Outcomes: What Determines India's Voting Behaviour?" *Economic and Political Weekly*, February 8, 2003.

Banducci, S. (2004) "Gender Inequality, Participation and Policy", Paper presented at the workshop 'Low turnout-does it matter'? *European Consortium for Political Research (ECPR), Joint Session Workshops,* Uppsala, 13-18, April.

Bartle, J., and Paolo Bellucci (2006) "Beyond Party Identification and Beyond." ECPR Workshop.http:www.essex.ac.uk/ecpr/events/jointsession/Nicosia/outlines/ws22.pdf.

Beckwoth, K. (2000) "Beyond Compare? Women's Movement in Comparative Perspective"? *European Journal of Political Research*, 37:431-68.

Benjamin I.Page and Calvin Jones. "Reciprocal Effects of Policy Preferences, Party Loyalties and the Vote". *American Political Science Review* 73 (1979), pp.1071-1089.

Blumberg, R. (1988) "Income Under Female Versus Male Control." *Journal of Family Issues,* Vol.9, pp.51-84.

Bobo, L., and F.D.Gillian. (1990) "Race, Sociopolitical Participation, and Black Empowerment." *American Political Science Review* 84 (2): 377-93.

Brady, H.E.,Verba,S., and K.L. Schlozman (1995) "Beyond SES: A Resource model of Political Participation." *American Political Science Review,* 89 (2), 271-294.

Campbell, D.E., and Christiana Wolbrecht. "See Jane Run: Women Politicians as Role Model for Adolescents." *The Journal of Politics,* Vol, N.2, May 2006, pp.233-247.

Center for the Study of Developing Societies (2004) "Methodology of National Election Study", *The Hindu,* Thursday, May 20.

D. Rajeshwari. "How Gendered was Women's Participation in Election 2004?" *Economic and Political Weekly,* December 18, 2004, 5431-5436.

David Hill (1981) "Political Culture on Female Political Representation." *Journal of Politics* 43 (1): 159-65.

Evans,G., and R. Anderson.(2004) "Do Issues Decide"? *CREST Working Paper,* Number 105, June.

Fiske, S.T., et al. (1990) "On the Varieties and Utilities of Political Expertise." *Social Cognition,* 8, 31-48.

Fiske, S.T., et al. (1983) "The Novice and the Expert: Knowledge Based Strategies in Political Cognition." *The Journal of Experimental Social Psychology.* 19: 381-400.

Galston, W.A. (2001) "Political Knowledge, Political Engagement and Civic Education." *Annual Review Political Science,* 4,217-234.

Gosselin, S. (2005) "How Mobilizing is the Local Context? Citizens Participation in Local Elections in Poland and Hungary (1998-2002)." Paper Presented at ECPR Joint Sessions of Workshops, Granada, 14-19, April.

Goswami, S. (2001) "Changing Electoral Trends", *Economic and Political Weekly,* May 12-18, Vol.XXXVI, No.19.

Gronlund, K., and Abo Akademi. (2005) 'Political Knowledge and the Internet.' Paper Presented at the XIV tri-annual Conference of the Nordic Political Association (NOPSA), University of Iceland, Reykjavik, 11-13 August 2005. http://registration.yourhost.is/nopsa2005/papers/Gronlund%20Political%20Knowledge%20and%20the%20Internet.pdf.

Hanks, M. (1981) "Youth, voluntary association and political socialization" *Social Forces*, 60(1), 211-223.

Hazarika, S.D. "Political Participation of Women and the Dilectics of 73rd Amendment", *The Indian Journal of Political Science,* Vol.LXVII,No. 2, April-June, 2006.

Hen, M.M.Weinstein., & D.Wring. (2002) "A generation apart? Youth and political participation in Britain." *British Journal of Politics and Intergenerational Relations*, 4, 2:167-192.

ICSSR, Report of 1975, *Towards Equality,* National Committee on Status of Women, Allied Publishers.

IDEA 'Voter Turnout from 1945 to 2000: A Global Report on Political Participation,' (3rd Edition), Stockholm International IDEA.

Inglehart, R., *et al.* (2001) "Gender Equality and Democracy." *Teaching and Research Review.* Issue 5, Winter 2005.

Inglehart, R.,& Pippa Norris. "The Development Theory of the Gender Gap: Women and Men's Voting Behavior in Global Perspective." *International Political Science Review*, May 15, 1999.

International IDEA. (2002) 'Women in Parliament.' Stockholm.http://www.idea.int.

International Parliamentary Union (1997) 'Men and Women in Politics.' Reports and Documents Series 28, IPU, Geneva.

International Parliamentary Union, Press Release, No.220, Geneva/New York, 27 February, 2006.

Joan Y.H. Leung (1991) "Political Orientations: Turnout and Vote Choice." *Asian Journal of Public Administration*, Vol.13, No.2, December, 55-87.

Johnston, R., *et al.,* "A Missing Level in the Analysis of a 1992-1997 Longitudinal Survey." ESRC Research Methods Programme, Working Paper No.3.

K.Joseph and Joel Westheimer. "The Limits of Political Efficacy: Educating Citizens for a Democratic Society." *Political Science and Politics*, Vol.XXXIX, Number 2, April 2006.

Kim,J.,Wyatt, R.O., & Katz,E. (1999) "News, talk, opinion, participation: The part played by conversation in deliberative democracy." *Political Communication,* 16,361-385.

Knack, S., & M. Kropf. (1998) "For Shame! The Effect of the Community Cooperation Context on the Probability of Voting." *Political Psychology* (19): 585-599.

Kondo, Norio. (2007) 'Election Studies in India.' Institute of Developing Economics, Discussion Paper No.98. March.http://www.ide.go.jp/English/Dp/pdf/098_kondo.pdf.

Krishna, A. (2002) "Enhancing Political Participation in Democracies—What is the Role of Social Capital?" *Comparative Political Studies,* 35 (4): 437-460, May.

Kunovich, S.,& Pamela Paxton. "Pathways to Power: The Role of Political Parties in Women's National Political Representation." *American Journal of Sociology,* Vol.111, Number 2, September 2005, 505-52.

Lake, R.L., & Robert Huckfeldt. (1998) "Social Capital, Social Networks and Political Participation." *Political Psychology,* 19:567-583.

Lawrence, C. (2001) The Evolution of Normal Vote in the 1990's. Paper Presented at the 2001 Annual Meeting of the Western Political Science Association, Las Vegas, Nevada 15-17 March.

Luskin, Robert C. (1990) "Explaining Political Sophistication". *Political Behaviour* 12:335.

Mahanta, A. "Political Empowerment of Women: Some Conceptual Issues." Vol.V. December 1998, *Journal of Politics.*

McLeod, J.,*et al.,* "Community Integration, local media use and democratic processes." *Communication Research,* Vol.23, 1996, pp.179-209.

Mehta, U. "Indian Women and their Participation in Politics." *Social Change,* Vol.8, No.3, September 1978.

Nagaland Post, Saturday, July 2, 2005.

National Readership Study.http://www.auditbureau.org/

Nevitte, N., *et al.* (2002) Socio-Economic Status and Non-Voting: A Comparative Cross-National Analysis. Paper Presented at the XVIIIth World Congress of the *International Political Science Association*, 1-5 August 2000, Quebec City, Canada.

Niemi, R.G., Craig, S.C., & F. Mattei. "Measuring Internal Political Efficacy in the 1988 National Election Study." *American Political Science Review*, 85 (4), 1991, 1407-1413.

Norris, P., & Inglehart. (2004) "Religious Organisations and Social Capital", *IJNL*, Vol.6, Issue 4, September.

Norris, P., & Inglehart. (2001) "Cultural Obstacles to Equal Representation," *Journal of Democracy* 12 (3): 127-140.

Page, I.B., & C. Jones. "Reciprocal Effects of Policy Preferences, Party Loyalties, and the Vote." *American Political Science Review* 73, 1979, pp.1071-1089.

Palshikar, S., & Sanjay Kumar. "Participatory Norm: How Broad Based is it?", *Economic and Political Weekly*, December 18, 2004.

Plutzer, E. "Becoming a Habitual Voter: Inertia, Resources and Growth in Young Adulthood." *American Political Science Review,* 96 (1), 2002,41-56.

"Psychological Involvement in Politics." *Election Archives and International Politics*, Vol.20, November-December 1989, p.68.

Racioppi, L., & Katherine O'Sullivan See. "Engendering Democratic Transition for Conflict: Women's Inclusion in North Ireland's Peace Process." *Comparative Politics*, Vol.38, Number 2, January 2006, p.193.

Richard, N., *et al.*, "Elections Campaigns as Information Campaigns: Who Learns What and with What Effect?" *American Political Science Review*, March 2001.

Robert, M Stein, J.Leighley,C.Owens. (2005) Who Votes, Who Does'nt, Why and, what can be done? A Report to the Federal Commission on Electoral Reform, June.http://www.American.edu/ia/cfer/0630test/stein.pdf.

Rosenstone, S.J. "Economic Adversity and Voting Turnout," *American Journal of Political Science,* 26, 1982, p.33.

Rubenson, D. "Can Social Capital Account for Differences in Political Participation across American Cities"? Paper

Delivered at the 2005 Annual Meeting of the American Political Science Association, September 1-4, Washington D.C. http://personal.Ise.ac.uk/rubenson/downloads/social%20capital.pdf.

Sapiro, V. (2000) "Political Participation: Building a Research Agenda" Paper Presented for the Conference on Center for the Study of Democratic Politics, October.

Sapiro, V. (2003) "Gender, Social Capital and Politics", Paper prepared for the Conference of Gender and Social Capital, University of Manitoba, Winnipeg, May.http://www.polisci.wisc.edu/users/sapiro/papers/vssoccap.pdf.

Schlozman, K.Lehman,N.Burns,S.Verba and J.Donahue. (1995) "Gender and Citizens Participation: Is there a Different Voice?" *American Journal of Political Science* 39 (2): 267-293.

Searing, D.D., *et al.,* (2004) Studying Everyday Talk in the Deliberative System: Does Democratic Discussion Make Better Citizens? Paper presented at the conference on "Empirical Approaches to Deliberative Politics" European University Institute, Swiss Chair Firenze, 21-22 May.

Shah, D.,McLeod, J., and Yoon, S. "Communication, Content and Community: An exploration of print, broadcast and internet influences." *Communication Research*, Vol.28, 2001, pp.464-506.

Strate, J.,M. Charles J. Parrish, C.D. Elder and C. Ford. (1989) "Life Span Civic Development and Voting Participation." *American Political Science Review*, Vol.83 (2): 443-464.

Susan, F.T., D.R.Kinder and W.M. Larter. (1983) "The Novice and the Expert: Knowledge Based Strategies in Political Cognition." *The Journal of Experimental Social Psychology,* 19:381-400.

Swanson, D. "The Homologous Evolution of Political Communication and Civic Engagement: Good News, Bad News and No News." *Political Communication*, Vol.17, 2000.

Thakkar, U. *Engendering Politics for Good Governance:* Advocacy By Women For Social and Political Change.

The Hindu, March 9, 1999.

USAID, *The Role of Media in Democracy: Strategic Approach*, Centre for Democracy and Governance, Bureau of Global Programs, Field Support and Research, Washington D.C, June 1999.

Verba, S. Would the dream of Political Equality Turn out to be a Nightmare? http//www.apsanet.org/ingtest/verba.pdf

Verba, S.,*et al.*, "Citizen's Activity: Who Participates? What Do They Say?" *American Political Science Review*, Vol.87, No.2, 1993, pp.303-318.

William R. Schonfeld. "The Meaning of Democratic Participation." *World Politics*, Vol.28, No.1, 1975, pp.134-158.

Zaller, J.R. "Political Awareness, elite opinion leadership and the mass survey response." *Social Cognition*, 8, 1990, 125-153.

Zipp, J.F., *et al.*, "Political Parties and Political Participation, A Reexamination of the Standard Socioeconomic Model." *Social Forces* 60, 1982, 1140-1153.

Index

W

Z

■■■